DAILY

DEVOTIONAL

FOR COUPLES

CONTENTS

INTRODUCTION

Welcome, dear couples, to a year-long journey of growing closer to God and to each other. This devotional isn't just another book to sit on your nightstand—it's a daily invitation to discover how God's Word speaks directly into your relationship.

Every marriage is a beautiful tapestry woven with threads of joy, challenge, laughter, and tears. Some days you'll feel perfectly in sync with your spouse; other days you might wonder if you're even speaking the same language. Through it all, God is present, offering wisdom, comfort, and guidance for every season of your relationship.

This devotional is designed to take just a few minutes each morning or evening. Read the scripture together, reflect on the devotion, and let the question at the end spark meaningful conversation. You don't need to be Bible scholars or have perfect faith—just come as you are, with open hearts.

Whether you're newlyweds figuring out how to merge two lives into one, or you've been married for decades and want to deepen your spiritual connection, these daily readings will meet you where you are. They're written in everyday language because God's truth isn't meant to be complicated—it's meant to be lived.

As you journey through these 365 days together, may you discover fresh mercies each morning, find strength for every challenge, and grow not just as individuals but as a couple rooted in God's unfailing love.

JANUARY: NEW BEGINNINGS TOGETHER

DAY 1

"Therefore shall a man leave his father and his mother, and shall cleave unto his wife: and they shall be one flesh." – Genesis 2:24 (KJV)

New Year's Day brings fresh starts and renewed hope. Just as January marks a new beginning on the calendar, your marriage is a continual opportunity for new beginnings. God designed marriage to be a leaving and cleaving—leaving behind old patterns and cleaving to something entirely new.

Think about how two rivers merge. At first, the waters swirl and clash, each maintaining its own current. But eventually, they flow as one powerful stream. Today, as you face a new year together, remember that becoming one doesn't mean losing yourselves—it means discovering who you can be together.

Reflection Question: What new beginning can you embrace together this year?

DAY 2

"This is the day which the Lord hath made; we will rejoice and be glad in it." – Psalm 118:24 (KJV)

Yesterday's mistakes don't have to define today's possibilities. Every morning, God gives you and your spouse a gift—24 fresh hours to love, forgive, and grow together. That argument from last night? It doesn't have to spill into breakfast. The disappointment from last week? Today offers a chance to heal.

Consider how the sun rises each morning regardless of how stormy yesterday was. God's mercies work the same way in your marriage. He doesn't recycle yesterday's grace; He provides brand new mercies tailored for today's needs.

Reflection Question: How can you help your spouse rejoice in this specific day God has made?

DAY 3

"And be ye kind one to another, tenderhearted, forgiving one another, even as God for Christ's sake hath forgiven you." – Ephesians 4:32 (KJV)

Kindness in marriage often shows up in the smallest gestures—making coffee just the way they like it, leaving an encouraging note, or simply asking "How can I help?" These tiny acts are like seeds that grow into a garden of trust and affection.

But here's what's harder: being kind when you don't feel like it. When they've left their socks on the floor again. When they forgot something important. That's when kindness becomes a choice, not just a feeling. It's choosing to see your spouse through God's eyes—flawed but deeply loved.

Reflection Question: What small act of kindness can you do today without being asked?

DAY 4

"Two are better than one; because they have a good reward for their labour." – Ecclesiastes 4:9 (KJV)

Have you ever tried to move a couch by yourself? You strain, you struggle, and usually end up stuck in a doorway. But with your spouse's help, what seemed impossible becomes manageable. Solomon understood this principle—life is simply better when shared.

Your marriage multiplies joy and divides sorrow. That promotion feels sweeter when you have someone to celebrate with. That loss feels lighter when someone shares the burden. You're not just roommates splitting rent; you're partners multiplying life's rewards.

Reflection Question: What burden can you help carry for your spouse today?

DAY 5

"Let all bitterness, and wrath, and anger, and clamour, and evil speaking, be put away from you." – Ephesians 4:31 (KJV)

Bitterness in marriage is like leaving milk out overnight—what starts small eventually spoils everything around it. Here's the thing about bitterness: it promises justice but delivers prison. You think you're punishing your spouse by holding onto hurt, but you're actually locking yourself in a cell of resentment. Meanwhile, your spouse might not even remember what they said.

God calls you to put it away—not tomorrow, not when they apologize properly, but now.

Reflection Question: What bitterness do you need to release before it spoils your marriage?

DAY 6

"Whoso findeth a wife findeth a good thing, and obtaineth favour of the Lord." – Proverbs 18:22 (KJV)

When was the last time you looked at your spouse and thought, "I found a good thing"? Not despite their quirks, but because of them. Marriage isn't about perfection—it's about seeing God's favor in the person He gave you. Your spouse is a blessing, an answer to prayers you didn't even pray. Yes, they may load the dishwasher "wrong" or squeeze toothpaste from the middle, but they're still God's gift to you. Today, focus less on irritations and more on the blessing. You didn't just find a spouse; you received divine favor.

Reflection Question: How can you show gratitude today for the "good thing" God gave you in your spouse?

DAY 7

"But seek ye first the kingdom of God, and his righteousness; and all these things shall be added unto you." – Matthew 6:33 (KJV)

Every couple juggles priorities—mortgage, kids, careers—but Jesus invites us to seek God's kingdom first. This doesn't mean neglecting responsibilities; it means aligning them under God's authority. Picture your marriage as a house: decorating and repairs are useless if the foundation cracks. God's kingdom is that foundation. Prioritizing Him together through prayer, worship, and service strengthens what holds everything up. Start small—five minutes of prayer over coffee can transform your day. When you seek Him first, you'll be amazed how "all these things" fall into place, aligning your marriage and life with His perfect plan.

Reflection Question: What's one way you can seek God's kingdom together before tackling today's to-do list?

DAY 8

"A soft answer turneth away wrath: but grievous words stir up anger." – *Proverbs 15:1 (KJV)*

Your spouse comes home frustrated, their tone sharp. You have two choices: fuel the fire with defensiveness or extinguish it with gentleness. A soft answer isn't weakness; it's wisdom. Harsh words often reflect a tough day, not you. Responding gently makes you a peacemaker, not a doormat. Next time tension rises, pause, breathe, and choose healing words over hurtful ones. Your marriage is too valuable to let harsh words cause damage. A gentle response can bring calm, showing love and preserving the bond you've built together.

Reflection Question: How can you prepare a soft answer for the next moment of tension?

DAY 9

"Bear ye one another's burdens, and so fulfil the law of Christ." – *Galatians 6:2 (KJV)*

Your spouse's burdens aren't just their struggles—they're your ministry. When they face work stress, family drama, or anxiety, God calls you to step in as a burden-bearer. This doesn't mean fixing everything. Sometimes it's listening without offering solutions, holding them while they cry, taking on extra chores, or praying when they can't. Christ carried our ultimate burden on the cross. By helping carry your spouse's load, even briefly, you're reflecting His love in a tangible, meaningful way.

Reflection Question: What burden is your spouse carrying that you could help lighten today?

DAY 10

"Let us not love in word, neither in tongue; but in deed and in truth." – 1 John 3:18 (KJV)

"I love you" loses meaning without action—it's like promising dinner but never cooking. God calls you to love in deed and truth, especially in marriage, where your spouse sees the real you. Real love shines in the little things: filling their gas tank unasked, watching their favorite show, or choosing them daily through actions, not just words. Your spouse needs to feel loved, not just hear it. Today, let your actions speak louder than words and show them the depth of your love in tangible ways.

Reflection Question: What action can demonstrate your love more powerfully than words today?

DAY 11

"For where your treasure is, there will your heart be also." – Matthew 6:21 (KJV)

Your calendar and bank statement reveal your priorities. If work gets your best hours and your spouse the leftovers, your heart might be divided. Jesus teaches that our hearts follow our investments. Strengthening your marriage doesn't require grand gestures—it's putting your phone down at dinner, saving energy for late-night talks, and valuing moments together over career ambitions. When you invest time, attention, and resources in your spouse, your heart will follow. Your marriage transforms from an obligation into a treasure worth cherishing.

Reflection Question: How can you invest in your spouse today in a way that shows they're your treasure?

DAY 12

"Let nothing be done through strife or vainglory; but in lowliness of mind let each esteem other better than themselves." – Philippians 2:3 (KJV)

Marriage isn't a competition—there's no reward for being "right." When you argue to win, you both lose. Paul calls you to a higher standard: consider your spouse more important than yourself. This doesn't mean losing your voice but approaching conflicts with, "How can we both win?" instead of "How can I prove my point?" It's prioritizing unity over victory and connection over correction. When you value your spouse above yourself, they often reciprocate. Mutual submission creates a loving cycle that transforms your marriage into a partnership built on respect and selflessness.

Reflection Question: In what area can you put your spouse's needs above your own today?

DAY 13

"A merry heart doeth good like a medicine: but a broken spirit drieth the bones." – Proverbs 17:22 (KJV)

When was the last time you laughed together—really laughed? Laughter is medicine for marriage, healing in ways serious talks can't. It reminds you that you're not just partners in responsibility but companions in joy. Life brings enough heaviness; let your home be a place of lightness. Celebrate silly moments, dance in the kitchen, or share that embarrassing story again. Laughter doesn't ignore problems—it keeps them from overshadowing your joy. Today, choose laughter. It's the medicine your marriage needs to thrive.

Reflection Question: What can you do today to bring laughter into your home?

DAY 14

"And above all things have fervent charity among yourselves: for charity shall cover the multitude of sins." – 1 Peter 4:8 (KJV)

Love covers. It doesn't broadcast your spouse's flaws or keep score of wrongs. Like a warm blanket on a cold night, love covers the imperfections of being human. This doesn't mean ignoring serious issues but offering grace for everyday missteps—forgotten errands, grumpy mornings, thoughtless words. Love covers. By covering your spouse's sins with love, you create a safe space for growth. They're free to become better because they're loved even at their worst.

Reflection Question: What imperfection in your spouse can you choose to cover with love today?

DAY 15

"Iron sharpeneth iron; so a man sharpeneth the countenance of his friend." – Proverbs 27:17 (KJV)

Marriage is God's refining process. Like iron sharpening iron, you and your spouse smooth each other's rough edges. Sometimes it creates sparks—that's normal. Sharpening isn't always comfortable, but it's necessary for growth.

Your spouse sees angles of your character you can't see. When they point out areas for growth, resist the urge to defend. They're not your enemy; they're your refiner. Similarly, when you see areas where they could grow, speak truth in love, not criticism.

The goal isn't to reshape your spouse into your image—it's allowing God to use you both as tools for mutual refinement.

Reflection Question: How can you receive your spouse's sharpening as a gift rather than an attack?

DAY 16

"Casting all your care upon him; for he careth for you." – *1 Peter 5:7 (KJV)*

You weren't meant to carry every worry about your marriage alone. Mortgage stress, parenting fears, health concerns—God invites you to cast them all on Him. Not just some, but all. Imagine standing with your spouse at a cliff's edge, holding bags of worries. God says, "Throw them over—I've got nets below you can't see." Casting your cares together is an act of faith, admitting you need His help. Tonight, instead of rehashing worries, pray together. Name each concern and hand it to God. He cares for you and your marriage more than you can imagine.

Reflection Question: What care can you and your spouse cast on God together today?

DAY 17

"The LORD is nigh unto them that are of a broken heart; and saveth such as be of a contrite spirit." – *Psalm 34:18 (KJV)*

Sometimes marriage breaks you—not in destruction, but in humbling. It reveals selfishness and stubbornness you didn't see before. This brokenness isn't failure; it's where God works best. When you and your spouse hit a wall—financially, emotionally, or spiritually—remember God draws near to broken hearts. He doesn't wait for you to fix it; He meets you in the mess, the tears, and the humble "we can't do this alone." Your broken places can become your strongest bonds when you allow God to heal them together.

Reflection Question: Where do you need God to draw near to your brokenness as a couple?

DAY 18

"Let no corrupt communication proceed out of your mouth, but that which is good to the use of edifying." – Ephesians 4:29 (KJV)

Words are seeds. Every conversation with your spouse plants either flowers or weeds. Criticism and complaints grow resentment, while encouragement and kindness bloom into love. Reflect on your last conversation—did your words build up or tear down? It's not about fake positivity but choosing words that construct rather than destroy. Your spouse faces enough criticism from the world; they need to be built up, especially by you. Let your words act as a construction crew, building their confidence and strengthening your bond, not a wrecking ball that tears it down.

Reflection Question: What words can you speak today to build up your spouse?

DAY 19

"Commit thy works unto the LORD, and thy thoughts shall be established." – Proverbs 16:3 (KJV)

Every couple has plans—vacations, retirement goals, parenting strategies. But Solomon reminds us: commit those plans to God, and your thoughts will align with His purposes. This doesn't guarantee everything will go as expected, but when you submit your plans to Him, He will either bless them or redirect them for your good. That house you want to buy? Commit it to Him. That job change you're considering? Give it to God first. By committing your works together, you acknowledge that God's plans are greater—and always better—than your own.

Reflection Question: What plan can you commit to God together before moving forward?

DAY 20

"Be not deceived; God is not mocked: for whatsoever a man soweth, that shall he also reap." – Galatians 6:7 (KJV)

Marriage is a garden where you reap what you sow. Plant neglect, and you'll harvest distance. Plant criticism, and you'll harvest resentment. But plant kindness, and you'll harvest intimacy. Plant patience, and you'll harvest trust. You can't plant thistles and expect roses. If your marriage feels distant, examine what you've been sowing—quality time or excuses? Forgiveness or scorekeeping? The good news is you can start planting differently today. Every loving gesture, kind word, and act of service is a seed. Be patient—harvests take time, but they always come.

Reflection Question: What seeds do you want to plant in your marriage today?

DAY 21

"Let us therefore come boldly unto the throne of grace, that we may obtain mercy, and find grace to help in time of need." – Hebrews 4:16 (KJV)

You don't need to have it all together before bringing your marriage to God. Come boldly with your mess, questions, and failures—His throne offers grace, not judgment. Maybe you've struggled with the same issue for years or feel like you're failing as a spouse. God says, "Come boldly anyway." He has mercy for your failures and grace for your needs. Praying together is an act of humility, admitting you need His help—and that's exactly where He works best. Don't wait for perfection. Come as you are, and let His grace transform what you bring.

Reflection Question: What need can you boldly bring to God's throne together?

DAY 22

"He that covereth a transgression seeketh love; but he that repeateth a matter separateth very friends." – Proverbs 17:9 (KJV)

How many times have you brought up that old hurt—the one you said you forgave? Rehashing past wounds is like picking at a scab; it prevents healing and leaves scars. Forgiveness doesn't mean pretending it didn't happen—it means choosing not to weaponize it later. True forgiveness buries the offense, rather than keeping it alive for convenience. Your spouse needs to know that forgiveness means freedom, not probation. By covering their transgressions, you're choosing love over leverage and creating space for healing and trust.

Reflection Question: What past hurt do you need to stop rehearsing and truly cover with love?

DAY 23

"For God hath not given us the spirit of fear; but of power, and of love, and of a sound mind." – 2 Timothy 1:7 (KJV)

Fear whispers lies to marriages: "What if they leave?" "What if we can't make it?" "What if we're failing?" But fear isn't from God. He's given you power, love, and a sound mind. When fear creeps in, recognize its source—it's not from Him. God equips you with power to overcome, love to strengthen your bond, and wisdom to make sound decisions. Face your fears together, but don't let them take control. Trust that God has already provided everything you need to build a strong, lasting marriage.

Reflection Question: What fear can you confront together with God's power, love, and sound mind?

DAY 24

"Delight thyself also in the LORD; and he shall give thee the desires of thine heart." – Psalm 37:4 (KJV)

When you delight in God together, your desires align with His will. You stop craving what harms your marriage and start longing for what strengthens it. God isn't a vending machine for wishes; instead, as you delight in Him, He shapes your desires to reflect His best for you. That dream you're chasing might shift, and the prayers you're praying may evolve. Make delighting in God a shared activity—worship, serve, and study His Word together. Over time, you'll see your hearts and desires harmonize in ways only He can orchestrate.

Reflection Question: How can you delight in the Lord together today?

DAY 25

"A friend loveth at all times, and a brother is born for adversity." – Proverbs 17:17 (KJV)

Your spouse should be your closest friend, not just your roommate or co-parent. Friends love at all times—morning breath and all, bad hair days included, grumpy moods accepted.

But notice the second part: born for adversity. When life hits hard, your spouse is designed by God to stand with you. They're not just there for date nights and anniversaries; they're equipped for emergencies and difficulties.

Nurture the friendship in your marriage. Play together, laugh together, share secrets. When adversity comes—and it will—you'll face it with your best friend.

Reflection Question: How can you strengthen the friendship aspect of your marriage today?

DAY 26

"And let us not be weary in well doing: for in due season we shall reap, if we faint not." – Galatians 6:9 (KJV)

Marriage is a marathon, not a sprint. Some days loving your spouse is easy; other days, it's exhausting. Paul encourages: don't grow weary—the harvest is coming. Maybe you've been patient without change, serving without recognition, or forgiving without transformation. Keep going. Due season isn't always tomorrow, but it's always coming. Each act of kindness—making coffee, speaking gently, offering grace—is building something beautiful. Don't give up now. Your harvest is closer than you realize.

Reflection Question: Where do you need encouragement to keep doing good in your marriage?

DAY 27

"Wherefore comfort yourselves together, and edify one another, even as also ye do." – 1 Thessalonians 5:11 (KJV)

Your spouse faces unseen battles—internal struggles, workplace pressures, family dynamics. God calls you to be their comforter and encourager, not their critic or coach. Comfort means holding them without fixing, validating their feelings even when you don't fully understand. Edifying means speaking life into their dreams, celebrating small wins, and believing in them when they can't believe in themselves. You have the power to be their safe haven in a harsh world. Use it generously.

Reflection Question: How can you comfort and edify your spouse in their current struggle?

DAY 28

"The heart of her husband doth safely trust in her, and she shall have no need of spoil." – Proverbs 31:11 (KJV)

Trust is the foundation of marriage. When your spouse can trust you—with secrets, failures, and dreams—your relationship becomes unshakeable. This trust isn't just about fidelity; it's emotional, spiritual, and practical reliability. Can your spouse trust you with their vulnerability? Do you support them in struggles or shame them? Trust is built in small moments but destroyed in seconds. Be the safe haven where your spouse's heart can rest. Guard their secrets, honor their vulnerability, and prove your trustworthiness every day.

Reflection Question: How can you show your spouse today that their heart is safe with you?

DAY 29

"And be not conformed to this world: but be ye transformed by the renewing of your mind." – Romans 12:2 (KJV)

The world says marriage should be easy, always romantic, and free of sacrifice. But God calls you to a higher standard—a transformed understanding of love. Stop comparing your marriage to social media highlights or Hollywood fantasies. Instead, let God renew your mind about real love: sacrifice, service, and steadfastness. It's beautiful, though not always glamorous. When you stop following the world's script and embrace God's design, transformation happens. Your expectations shift from perfection to growth, from ease to purpose.

Reflection Question: What worldly marriage expectation do you need to release?

DAY 30

"Finally, brethren, whatsoever things are true, whatsoever things are honest, whatsoever things are just, whatsoever things are pure, whatsoever things are lovely, whatsoever things are of good report; if there be any virtue, and if there be any praise, think on these things." – Philippians 4:8 (KJV)

Your thoughts about your spouse shape your marriage more than you realize. Fixating on their flaws makes them seem bigger, but focusing on their strengths allows love to grow. Make a mental list: What's true, good, and lovely about your spouse? What virtues do they have? This isn't denying problems—it's choosing to focus on the positive while addressing challenges. Your mind is powerful. Use it to build your marriage by dwelling on what's praiseworthy.

Reflection Question: What praiseworthy quality in your spouse can you focus on today?

DAY 31

"Trust in the LORD with all thine heart; and lean not unto thine own understanding." – Proverbs 3:5 (KJV)

As January ends, you may be reflecting on your marriage goals. Here's God's advice: trust Him more than your own understanding. Your perspective is limited; His is eternal. Maybe your marriage isn't where you hoped it would be, or unexpected challenges arose. Don't rely on how things "should" look—trust that God is working, even when it's unseen. Your marriage is safest in His capable hands. He sees the full picture—past, present, and future. Lean into His wisdom, not your worry.

Reflection Question: Where do you need to trust God's plan for your marriage over your own understanding?

FEBRUARY: LOVE IN ACTION

DAY 32

"Many waters cannot quench love, neither can the floods drown it." – Song of Solomon 8:7 (KJV)

February celebrates love, but real love isn't just Valentine's cards and chocolate. It's the love that survives floods—financial crisis, health scares, family drama. This love doesn't just endure; it emerges stronger.

Think of your love like a flame. Rain might make it flicker, but it can't extinguish what God has ignited. Those "many waters" you're facing—stress, disagreements, disappointments—they're testing your love, not destroying it.

Your love story isn't written in perfect moments but in perseverance through imperfect ones. The floods will come, but your love is designed to outlast them all.

Reflection Question: What flood are you facing that needs unquenchable love?

DAY 33

"Beloved, let us love one another: for love is of God; and every one that loveth is born of God, and knoweth God." – 1 John 4:7 (KJV)

Your ability to love your spouse doesn't depend on feelings—it flows from God. When feelings fade (and they will at times), you can still love because you're connected to the Source. This is freeing: you don't have to produce love from an empty well. God's love flows through you to your spouse. When loving feels hard, draw closer to Him and let Him fill you. Your marriage is a conduit for God's love. Keep the channel clear through prayer, worship, and surrender.

Reflection Question: How can you better connect to God's love to flow through you to your spouse?

DAY 34

"Greater love hath no man than this, that a man lay down his life for his friends." – John 15:13 (KJV)

Laying down your life for your spouse rarely looks like dramatic sacrifice. It looks like giving up your Saturday golf to help with house projects. It's choosing their restaurant when you're craving something else. It's dying to selfishness in a thousand small ways.

Every time you choose your spouse over yourself, you're practicing this greater love. It's not about losing yourself—it's about finding joy in their happiness, peace in their comfort, satisfaction in their success.

This sacrificial love isn't weakness; it's the strongest force in marriage. It breaks down walls and builds bridges.

Reflection Question: What can you lay down today for your spouse's benefit?

DAY 35

"Set me as a seal upon thine heart, as a seal upon thine arm: for love is strong as death." – Song of Solomon 8:6 (KJV)

A seal in ancient times meant ownership and protection. Your spouse should be sealed on your heart—marked as yours, protected from rivals, secured in position. This isn't possessiveness; it's covenant commitment.

Love that's strong as death doesn't give up when things get difficult. It doesn't look for escape routes or keep one foot out the door. It seals the exits and says, "We're working this out together."

In a world of disposable relationships, be sealed to each other. Let your love be the kind that death alone can separate.

Reflection Question: How can you demonstrate that your spouse is sealed upon your heart?

DAY 36

"Love suffereth long, and is kind; love envieth not; love vaunteth not itself, is not puffed up." – 1 Corinthians 13:4 (KJV)

Love is patient when your spouse needs reminders. It's kind when they're not at their best. It doesn't envy their successes or compete for attention but celebrates them. Love isn't just a feeling—it's a choice. You can choose patience when frustrated, kindness when hurt, and humility even when you're right. Today, take one aspect of love from this verse and practice it intentionally. Let love be your action, not just your emotion.

Reflection Question: Which aspect of love from this verse does your marriage need most today?

DAY 37

"Hatred stirreth up strifes: but love covereth all sins." – Proverbs 10:12 (KJV)

Love is a blanket that covers the small irritations in marriage, shielding faults from scrutiny and mistakes from judgment. It doesn't ignore serious issues but chooses not to overreact to minor offenses. They forgot to call? Love covers. They were thoughtless or disappointing? Love covers and responds with grace. By generously covering your spouse's small flaws, you create a safe space for growth and change, fostering trust and connection.

Reflection Question: What irritation can you choose to cover with love rather than expose?

DAY 38

"Nevertheless let every one of you in particular so love his wife even as himself; and the wife see that she reverence her husband." – Ephesians 5:33 (KJV)

This isn't about outdated roles—it's about meeting deep needs. Husbands need respect like oxygen; wives need love like water. When you understand your spouse's primary emotional need, you can love them more effectively.

Love looks like security, cherishing, and emotional connection. Respect looks like admiration, trust, and honoring their decisions. Both require intentionality. You might naturally give what you want to receive, but wisdom gives what your spouse needs most.

Study your spouse. Learn their love language. Give them what fills their tank, not what fills yours.

Reflection Question: How can you better meet your spouse's unique emotional needs today?

DAY 39

"By this shall all men know that ye are my disciples, if ye have love one to another." – John 13:35 (KJV)

Your marriage is a testimony. The way you love each other preaches louder than any sermon. When others see how you treat each other—with patience, kindness, respect—they see Jesus.

This puts your marriage in eternal perspective. It's not just about your happiness; it's about His glory. The way you forgive, serve, and sacrifice for each other points others to Christ.

Your love story is part of God's larger story. Make it one that draws others to Him.

Reflection Question: What does your marriage teach others about God's love?

DAY 40

"There is no fear in love; but perfect love casteth out fear." – 1 John 4:18 (KJV)

Fear corrupts marriage—fear of rejection, vulnerability, or failure. But perfect love creates perfect safety, dissolving fear. Build an atmosphere where fears can be shared without judgment. When your spouse admits a fear, don't minimize or rush to fix it. Gently hold it, like a fragile bird, and let love bring healing. Perfect love isn't about flawless performance; it's about consistent, unconditional acceptance that makes fear unnecessary.

Reflection Question: What fear in your marriage needs to be cast out by perfect love?

DAY 41

"And Jacob served seven years for Rachel; and they seemed unto him but a few days, for the love he had to her." – Genesis 29:20 (KJV)

Love changes how we perceive time. Jacob's seven years felt like days because love made the waiting worthwhile. In marriage, love shortens difficult seasons and makes sweet moments linger. Whether you're saving for a house, raising children, or facing challenges, love makes the journey bearable—and even joyful. The destination matters less than who you're traveling with. Don't wish away hard seasons; instead, find love in them. Through love's lens, they'll seem like "but a few days."

Reflection Question: How can love help you reframe a current challenging season?

DAY 42

"Charity suffereth long, and is kind." – 1 Corinthians 13:4 (KJV)

Suffering long doesn't mean being a martyr. It means having patient endurance when change comes slowly. Your spouse might take years to overcome that habit, heal from that wound, or learn that lesson. Love waits without keeping score.

But notice—it's kind while waiting. Not bitter, not resentful, not passive-aggressive. Patient love speaks truth gently, maintains hope consistently, and celebrates small progress enthusiastically.

Your spouse is under construction, just like you. Be patient with their progress and kind in their process.

Reflection Question: Where do you need to practice long-suffering kindness with your spouse?

DAY 43

"Let love be without dissimulation." – Romans 12:9 (KJV)

Fake love is exhausting—pretending everything's fine when it's not, performing happiness for others while dying inside. God calls for love without dissimulation—genuine, authentic, real.

This means being honest about struggles while remaining committed to growth. It's admitting when you don't feel loving but choosing love anyway. It's dropping the masks and being real with each other.

Authentic love isn't always pretty, but it's always powerful. It says, "I see the real you and choose you anyway."

Reflection Question: Where has your love become performance rather than authentic?

DAY 44

"Her children arise up, and call her blessed; her husband also, and he praiseth her." – Proverbs 31:28 (KJV)

When did you last praise your spouse publicly? Not just a casual compliment, but genuine praise that makes others see their value? Public praise does something private compliments can't—it declares your choice.

Praising your spouse to others—to your children, friends, family—builds their reputation and confidence. It tells the world, "This is my person, and I'm proud of them." It's choosing to be their biggest cheerleader, not their biggest critic.

Make praise your default setting. Catch them doing something right and announce it.

Reflection Question: How can you publicly praise your spouse today?

DAY 45

"And though I have the gift of prophecy, and understand all mysteries, and all knowledge; and though I have all faith, so that I could remove mountains, and have not charity, I have nothing." – 1 Corinthians 13:2 (KJV)

You could be the perfect spouse on paper—providing, keeping the house spotless, remembering anniversaries—but without love, it's just performance. Love isn't about the actions; it's the heart behind them. Your spouse needs more than your service—they need your affection. They need more than your provision—they need your presence. Right actions without love feel hollow. Check your motivation: are you serving from love or obligation? The same actions flow differently depending on the source.

Reflection Question: What marriage duty needs to be transformed by love?

DAY 46

"Love not in word, neither in tongue; but in deed and in truth." – 1 John 3:18 (KJV)

Words matter, but actions matter more. "I love you" needs feet—doing the dishes when they're exhausted, getting up with the baby so they can sleep, choosing their happiness over your convenience. Truth in love means your actions match your words consistently. Your spouse shouldn't have to wonder if you mean what you say. Your deeds should be the evidence of your declarations. Today, let your love walk, not just talk. Show what your words have been saying.

Reflection Question: What deed can demonstrate the love you've been speaking?

DAY 47

"We love him, because he first loved us." – 1 John 4:19 (KJV)

You can love your spouse because God loved you first. When you were unloveable, He loved you. When you were far from perfect, He pursued you. This is your model for marriage.

Don't wait for your spouse to earn your love or meet your standards. Love them because God loved you at your worst. Love first, love freely, love without conditions—just as you've been loved.

God's love for you is the well from which your love for your spouse flows. Keep drawing from it.

Reflection Question: How does God's love for you inspire your love for your spouse?

DAY 48

"And walk in love, as Christ also hath loved us, and hath given himself for us." – Ephesians 5:2 (KJV)

Walking in love is different from falling in love. Falling is passive; walking is intentional. Every day, you choose to take another step in love's direction, even when the path gets steep.

Christ's love led Him to give Himself completely. Your walk in love might mean giving up your preferences, your rights, your need to be right. It's daily choosing sacrifice over selfishness.

Love isn't a feeling you fall into; it's a path you walk together, one deliberate step at a time.

Reflection Question: What step in love do you need to take today?

DAY 49

"If a man say, I love God, and hateth his brother, he is a liar: for he that loveth not his brother whom he hath seen, how can he love God whom he hath not seen?" – 1 John 4:20 (KJV)

Your love for God is measured by your love for your spouse. It's easy to love an invisible God who doesn't leave socks on the floor. It's harder to love the visible person who does.

Your spouse is your closest neighbor, your most intimate brother or sister in Christ. How you treat them reveals your true spiritual condition. You can't claim to love God while harboring resentment toward the one sharing your bed.

Let your marriage be the proving ground for your faith. Love God by loving your spouse well.

Reflection Question: How does loving your spouse reflect your love for God?

DAY 50

"This is my commandment, That ye love one another, as I have loved you." – John 15:12 (KJV)

Jesus doesn't suggest love; He commands it. In marriage, love isn't optional or based on feelings—it's a direct order from your Commander-in-Chief. "As I have loved you" sets the standard impossibly high: sacrificial, unconditional, and persistent. You won't love perfectly, but you're called to try daily for Christ-like love. When love feels impossible, remember it's a command backed by divine enablement. God never commands what He won't empower.

Reflection Question: How can you obey the command to love your spouse today?

DAY 51

"Who can find a virtuous woman? for her price is far above rubies." –
Proverbs 31:10 (KJV)

Value isn't determined by perfection but by virtue. Your spouse's worth isn't in never making mistakes but in their character, faithfulness, and heart. They're more precious than any earthly treasure.

When you treat your spouse as valuable, they begin to see their own worth. Your perspective shapes their self-perception. See them as God does—precious, chosen, worth pursuing.

Stop comparing your ruby to other stones. You've been given a treasure; treat them accordingly.

Reflection Question: How can you show your spouse they're valued above rubies?

DAY 52

"My beloved is mine, and I am his." – Song of Solomon 2:16 (KJV)

Belonging to each other is both privilege and responsibility. You're not just roommates sharing expenses; you belong to each other in a way you belong to no one else.

This mutual belonging means your decisions affect each other. Your moods impact each other. Your victories and defeats are shared. You're intertwined by divine design.

Celebrate this belonging. In a world of independence, you've chosen beautiful interdependence.

Reflection Question: How can you celebrate belonging to each other today?

DAY 53

"Let the husband render unto the wife due benevolence: and likewise also the wife unto the husband." – 1 Corinthians 7:3 (KJV)

Benevolence in marriage means consistent kindness, goodwill, and assuming the best of your spouse's intentions. It's giving the benefit of the doubt when actions confuse you. This "due benevolence" isn't earned but owed because of the covenant you share. Kindness, patience, and grace are given not for performance but for promise. Offer your spouse what's due—not grudgingly, but generously. Benevolence fosters an atmosphere where love thrives.

Reflection Question: What benevolence does your spouse need from you today?

DAY 54

"Be kindly affectioned one to another with brotherly love; in honour preferring one another." – Romans 12:10 (KJV)

Preferring your spouse means putting them in the spotlight while you hold the ladder. It's celebrating their promotion even if yours was passed over. It's choosing their comfort over your convenience.

This isn't about becoming invisible; it's about making love visible through preference. When you consistently prefer your spouse, you create a cycle—they begin preferring you too.

Honor your spouse by putting them first in small, daily decisions. Watch how preference transforms your relationship.

Reflection Question: In what decision today can you prefer your spouse's choice?

DAY 55

"Let all that ye do be done with charity." – 1 Corinthians 16:14 (KJV)

Everything—from major decisions to mundane tasks—should be filtered through love. Making dinner? Do it with love. Discussing finances? Let love guide. Disciplining children? Love should be the foundation.

When love motivates everything, even difficult conversations become constructive. Criticism becomes coaching. Conflict becomes opportunity for deeper understanding.

Don't compartmentalize love for special occasions. Let it saturate every interaction, every decision, every ordinary moment.

Reflection Question: What routine task can you transform by doing it with love?

DAY 56

"Love worketh no ill to his neighbour: therefore love is the fulfilling of the law." – Romans 13:10 (KJV)

Love protects your spouse from harm—including harm from you. It refuses to wound with words, manipulate with emotions, or punish with silence. Love actively works for good, never ill.

This means checking your motives. Will this comment help or hurt? Will this action build or break? Love chooses construction over destruction every time.

You fulfill God's law in your marriage not through perfect performance but through persistent love that works no ill.

Reflection Question: How can you actively work good, not ill, for your spouse today?

DAY 57

"Keep yourselves in the love of God, looking for the mercy of our Lord Jesus Christ." – Jude 1:21 (KJV)

Keeping yourself in God's love isn't passive—it requires intentional positioning. Like staying under an umbrella in rain, you must choose to remain under love's covering.

In marriage, this means continually returning to love's source. When you drift toward irritation, reposition under God's love. When frustration builds, remember Christ's mercy toward you.

You can't give what you don't have. Keep yourself filled with God's love, and you'll have plenty to pour out.

Reflection Question: How can you better position yourself in God's love today?

DAY 58

"Husbands, love your wives, even as Christ also loved the church, and gave himself for it." – Ephesians 5:25 (KJV)

Christ's love for the church wasn't theoretical—it cost Him everything. This sacrificial love is the model for marriage: giving when tired, serving when unappreciated, and forgiving when hurt. Both spouses are called to this love, which doesn't keep score or demand equal returns but finds reward in giving itself. Your marriage needs this kind of love—not occasionally, but consistently. Give yourself to your spouse as Christ gave Himself for you.

Reflection Question: What sacrifice can you make for your spouse's benefit today?

DAY 59

"Beloved, if God so loved us, we ought also to love one another." – 1 John 4:11 (KJV)

The logic is simple: loved people love people. Since God loved you with infinite, unconditional love, you have no excuse for withholding love from your spouse.

This "ought" isn't guilt-driven but grace-driven. You love because you've been loved. You forgive because you've been forgiven. You show mercy because mercy was shown to you.

Let God's love for you be the foundation of your love for your spouse. The more you grasp His love, the more you'll have to give.

Reflection Question: How does experiencing God's love empower you to love your spouse?

BONUS DAY (LEAP YEAR)

"And now abideth faith, hope, charity, these three; but the greatest of these is charity." – 1 Corinthians 13:13 (KJV)

Faith believes the best about your marriage's future. Hope maintains vision when circumstances look dark. But love—love is the greatest because it acts regardless of faith's strength or hope's brightness.

Your marriage needs all three, but love leads. When faith wavers, love stands firm. When hope dims, love keeps serving. Love doesn't wait for perfect conditions; it creates them.

This bonus day reminds you that love is always the answer, always the way forward, always God's best for your marriage.

Reflection Question: How can you make love the greatest force in your marriage?

MARCH: GROWING TOGETHER

DAY 60

"To every thing there is a season, and a time to every purpose under the heaven." – Ecclesiastes 3:1 (KJV)

March brings spring's promise—dormant things beginning to stir. Your marriage has seasons too. Maybe you're in winter, where everything feels frozen and distant. Or perhaps you're experiencing summer's warmth, where connection comes easily.

Here's the secret: every season serves a purpose. Winter's cold drives roots deeper. Spring's rain brings growth. Summer's heat produces fruit. Fall's letting go makes room for new life. That difficult season you're in? It's not permanent, and it's not pointless.

Stop fighting your current season and start asking, "What's this teaching us?" Growth happens when you work with your season, not against it.

Reflection Question: What purpose might God have in your marriage's current season?

DAY 61

"Can two walk together, except they be agreed?" – Amos 3:3 (KJV)

Ever tried walking while tied to someone going a different direction? You'll either trip, argue, or stand still. Marriage works the same way—you need agreement on direction, even if you disagree on details.

Agreement doesn't mean identical opinions. It means shared values, common goals, unified purpose. You might debate the route, but you agree on the destination. You might have different methods, but you share the mission.

Find your common ground today. What do you both want for your marriage, your family, your future? Start there, and the steps become clearer.

Reflection Question: Where do you need to find agreement to walk together better?

DAY 62

"I am the vine, ye are the branches: He that abideth in me, and I in him, the same bringeth forth much fruit." – John 15:5 (KJV)

A branch disconnected from the vine looks fine for a while but eventually withers. Marriage works the same—disconnected from God, you may maintain appearances briefly, but you'll wither over time. Staying connected is simple: pray together, even a short "Thank you for this day," read scripture together, even one verse, or worship together, even by singing in the car. These small acts keep life flowing through your marriage. Without Him, you're just two people trying hard; with Him, you naturally bear fruit.

Reflection Question: How can you better connect to the Vine together today?

DAY 63

"A threefold cord is not quickly broken." – Ecclesiastes 4:12 (KJV)

You + your spouse = two cords. Strong, but not unbreakable. You + your spouse + God = a threefold cord. Now you're talking about serious strength. God isn't an add-on to your marriage; He's the third strand that makes it unbreakable.

When you're weak, your spouse might be strong. When you're both weak, God's strength holds everything together. That argument that feels marriage-ending? God's strand keeps you bound. That season where you feel more like roommates? His presence maintains connection.

Stop trying to be a strong two-cord marriage. Invite God into the center and become unbreakable.

Reflection Question: How can you strengthen God's strand in your marriage cord?

DAY 64

"And the Lord God said, It is not good that the man should be alone." – Genesis 2:18 (KJV)

Before sin or complications, God declared aloneness "not good." You were designed for partnership, and that need for connection isn't weakness—it's divine design. Marriage can feel lonelier than singleness when you're together but disconnected. Proximity doesn't cure emotional absence; you can share a bed but not your hearts. God's solution to aloneness is true companionship. Bridge the gap today: put down the phone, turn toward each other, and share something real. You were made for togetherness.

Reflection Question: Where has aloneness crept into your togetherness?

DAY 65

"Except the Lord build the house, they labour in vain that build it." – Psalm 127:1 (KJV)

You can build your marriage with the finest materials—communication techniques, date nights, counseling. All good things. But without God as the architect and builder, you're building on sand. This doesn't diminish your effort; it directs it. Work on your marriage, but know lasting strength requires the Master Builder. Every strong marriage shares the same foundation: God's presence and principles. Build on anything else, and the first storm will reveal the cracks.

Reflection Question: What area of your marriage needs God's building touch?

DAY 66

"But grow in grace, and in the knowledge of our Lord and Saviour Jesus Christ." – 2 Peter 3:18 (KJV)

Growth is the goal, not perfection. Your spouse doesn't need you to be flawless; they need you to be growing. Grace makes room for growth—yours and theirs. Picture two trees planted side by side. They grow at different rates and in unique ways, but together their roots intertwine, and their branches provide mutual shelter. That's marriage—growing individually yet together. Celebrate every step forward. Did your spouse handle stress better than last month? Growth. Did you hold your tongue when triggered? Growth. These small inches of progress add up to miles over time.

Reflection Question: What growth can you celebrate in your marriage this month?

DAY 67

"Let us not therefore judge one another any more: but judge this rather, that no man put a stumblingblock or an occasion to fall in his brother's way." – Romans 14:13 (KJV)

That thing your spouse does that drives you crazy? Maybe it's not worth the fight. Paul suggests judging something else—whether you're creating stumbling blocks for your spouse.

Are your expectations so high they're constantly failing? Is your criticism so frequent they've stopped trying? Sometimes the problem isn't their behavior but your response to it.

Remove stumbling blocks today. Lower the bar on perfection. Raise the bar on grace. Make it easier for your spouse to succeed.

Reflection Question: What stumbling block can you remove from your spouse's path?

DAY 68

"For where envying and strife is, there is confusion and every evil work." – James 3:16 (KJV)

Comparison is marriage poison. Envying another couple's highlight reel while living your behind-the-scenes breeds strife. "Why can't we be like them?" turns into "Why aren't you like that?" Strife invites confusion, turning small issues into major battles and leaving love lost in a fog of competition. But your marriage is unique. Stop comparing your chapter three to someone else's chapter twenty. Focus on writing your own story.

Reflection Question: What comparison do you need to release to reduce strife?

DAY 69

"But he that is greatest among you shall be your servant." – Matthew 23:11
(KJV)

Want to be great in your marriage? Serve. Not grudgingly, not for points, but genuinely. Greatness isn't measured by who wins arguments but by who serves most freely.

Service looks like getting up to get them water without being asked. It's handling that chore they hate. It's putting their preferences first without keeping score. This isn't doormat behavior—it's kingdom behavior.

Jesus modeled greatness through service. Your marriage needs that same servant-hearted love.

Reflection Question: How can you serve your spouse without expectation today?

DAY 70

"Death and life are in the power of the tongue." – Proverbs 18:21 (KJV)

Your words are creating something in your marriage—either life or death. That sarcastic comment? It's killing something. That word of encouragement? It's bringing life.

Think of words like seeds. Every conversation plants something that will eventually grow. Criticism grows resentment. Appreciation grows affection. Complaints grow distance. Gratitude grows intimacy.

You're either speaking life or death into your marriage today. There's no neutral. Choose your words like you're choosing your future—because you are.

Reflection Question: What life-giving words does your spouse need to hear?

DAY 71

"Be ye therefore merciful, as your Father also is merciful." – Luke 6:36 (KJV)

Mercy sees failure but chooses compassion. Your spouse will mess up—forget things, say hurtful words, make poor decisions. Mercy responds with grace, not judgment. God's mercy toward you is the model: He sees your worst and loves you still, knowing your failures yet extending grace. That's the mercy your marriage needs—seeing clearly but loving deeply. Mercy doesn't ignore problems; it addresses them with compassion, not condemnation.

Reflection Question: Where does your spouse need your mercy today?

DAY 72

"And let us consider one another to provoke unto love and to good works." – Hebrews 10:24 (KJV)

Provoke usually sounds negative, but here it's beautiful—deliberately stirring up love and good works in your spouse. You know their buttons; push the right ones.

What inspires your spouse to love better? What encourages their best self? Maybe it's affirming their efforts, celebrating their strengths, or believing in their dreams. Be intentional about provoking their best.

You have incredible influence over your spouse's growth. Use it to draw out their greatness, not their defensiveness.

Reflection Question: How can you provoke your spouse to love and good works?

DAY 73

"Likewise, ye younger, submit yourselves unto the elder. Yea, all of you be subject one to another, and be clothed with humility." – 1 Peter 5:5 (KJV)

Mutual submission means both yielding, serving, and choosing humility. It's not about control but about putting each other first—like a dance where both partners take turns leading and following. Humility in marriage looks like admitting when you're wrong, asking for help, and celebrating your spouse's victories without jealousy. It's wearing grace, not pride. When both embrace humility, power struggles fade, and you stop competing, instead completing each other.

Reflection Question: How can you clothe yourself with humility in your marriage today?

DAY 74

"A man's heart deviseth his way: but the Lord directeth his steps." – Proverbs 16:9 (KJV)

You've made plans together—financial goals, parenting strategies, career moves. Good! But hold them loosely. God might redirect your steps toward something better than you planned.

That unexpected job loss might lead to a better opportunity. That failed pregnancy attempt might precede a miracle. That financial setback might teach dependence on God. Your plans matter, but God's direction matters more.

Plan together, but surrender those plans to God's direction. His detours often lead to better destinations.

Reflection Question: What plan do you need to hold more loosely, trusting God's direction?

DAY 75

"My little children, let us not love in word, neither in tongue; but in deed and in truth." – 1 John 3:18 (KJV)

Talk is cheap in marriage. "I love you" becomes white noise without accompanying action. Your spouse needs to feel loved, not just hear about it.

Love in deed means doing the dishes without being asked. Love in truth means following through on promises. It's showing up tired but present, choosing connection over convenience, proving love through consistency.

Today, let your love walk around the house, visible and tangible.

Reflection Question: What deed can demonstrate your love more than words today?

DAY 76

"Wherefore, my beloved brethren, let every man be swift to hear, slow to speak, slow to wrath." – James 1:19 (KJV)

The formula for marital peace: quick ears, slow mouth, slower temper. Conflicts escalate when we reverse this—slow to hear, quick to speak, swift to anger. Truly hearing your spouse means listening to understand, not just to respond. It's hearing their heart, not just their words. Being slow to speak gives wisdom time to catch up with emotion. Practice the pause—count to five before responding. Listen for what's unsaid. Your marriage needs more listening and less lecturing.

Reflection Question: How can you be swifter to hear your spouse today?

DAY 77

"He that handleth a matter wisely shall find good." – Proverbs 16:20 (KJV)

Wisdom in marriage isn't about being right—it's about handling matters well. That disagreement about money? Handle it wisely. That recurring argument? Approach it differently.

Wise handling means choosing your battles, timing difficult conversations well, and approaching problems as teammates, not opponents. It's asking "How can we solve this?" instead of "Why did you do that?"

Every matter in your marriage can be handled wisely or foolishly. Choose wisdom, find good.

Reflection Question: What matter in your marriage needs wiser handling?

DAY 78

"For we walk by faith, not by sight." – 2 Corinthians 5:7 (KJV)

Some days, your marriage won't look promising. You'll see problems, not potential. Flaws, not beauty. Distance, not connection. That's when faith becomes essential.

Faith sees your spouse becoming who God designed them to be. Faith believes your marriage is worth fighting for even when feelings fade. Faith trusts God's working even when you can't see it.

Stop walking by what you see—circumstances, failures, disappointments. Start walking by faith in what God can do.

Reflection Question: Where do you need to walk by faith rather than sight in your marriage?

DAY 79

"Let no man despise thy youth; but be thou an example of the believers, in word, in conversation, in charity, in spirit, in faith, in purity." – 1 Timothy 4:12 (KJV)

Whatever stage your marriage is in—newlywed or seasoned—be an example. Young marriages can teach passion. Mature marriages can model perseverance. Every marriage has something to offer.

Don't wait until you're "perfect" to be an example. Your struggles and victories, your failures and recoveries—they all teach others. Your marriage is a living testimony of God's grace.

Be intentional about modeling healthy marriage. Others are watching and learning from your example.

Reflection Question: What example is your marriage setting for others?

DAY 80

"But the fruit of the Spirit is love, joy, peace, longsuffering, gentleness, goodness, faith, meekness, temperance." – Galatians 5:22-23 (KJV)

This isn't a multiple-choice list—all these fruits should grow in your marriage. Love without joy feels like duty, peace without patience becomes fragile, and gentleness without self-control is inconsistent. The Spirit produces the fruit, but your role is to cultivate growth by staying connected to God, pruning bad habits, and fostering spiritual growth. Examine your marriage orchard: which fruits are thriving, and which need care? The Spirit is ready to produce—are you ready to cultivate?

Reflection Question: Which spiritual fruit needs more cultivation in your marriage?

DAY 81

"Submit yourselves therefore to God. Resist the devil, and he will flee from you." – James 4:7 (KJV)

Your marriage has an enemy, and it's not each other. The real enemy wants division, distrust, and destruction. But here's the strategy: submit to God first, then resist together.

When you're submitted to God, you're positioned for victory. The enemy flees from marriages that are surrendered to God's authority. Unity under God creates an impenetrable defense.

Stop fighting each other and start fighting for your marriage. Submit together, resist together, win together.

Reflection Question: What attack on your marriage do you need to resist together?

DAY 82

"And he said unto me, My grace is sufficient for thee: for my strength is made perfect in weakness." – 2 Corinthians 12:9 (KJV)

Your weaknesses in marriage aren't disqualifiers—they're opportunities for God's strength. Can't communicate well? God's grace is sufficient. Struggle with patience? His strength perfects your weakness.

Stop hiding your weaknesses from your spouse. They already know them anyway. Instead, invite God's strength into those weak places. Let your spouse see you depending on God, not pretending perfection.

Your marriage doesn't need two strong people. It needs two people who know where their strength comes from.

Reflection Question: What weakness needs God's sufficient grace in your marriage?

DAY 83

"Be not wise in thine own eyes: fear the Lord, and depart from evil." –
Proverbs 3:7 (KJV)

"I know what's best for our marriage" might be the most dangerous thought. When you're wise in your own eyes, you stop seeking God's wisdom. Pride blinds you to your own contribution to problems.

Fearing the Lord in marriage means recognizing He knows better than you do. It's seeking His perspective on your conflicts, His wisdom for decisions, His way forward when you're stuck. Depart from the evil of self-reliance. Your own wisdom isn't enough for marriage's complexities.

Reflection Question: Where have you been too wise in your own eyes?

DAY 84

"Let your speech be always with grace, seasoned with salt." – Colossians 4:6
(KJV)

Grace makes words palatable; salt makes them memorable. Your speech needs both. Grace without salt is bland—nice but forgettable. Salt without grace is harsh—memorable but wounding.

Seasoned speech in marriage speaks truth lovingly. It addresses issues without attacking character. It's honest but kind, direct but gentle. Like a perfectly seasoned meal, it satisfies without overwhelming.

Before speaking, ask: Is this gracious? Will it preserve or corrode? Season your words well.

Reflection Question: How can you better season your speech with grace and salt?

DAY 85

"Whatsoever thy hand findeth to do, do it with thy might." – Ecclesiastes 9:10 (KJV)

Half-hearted effort in marriage yields half-hearted results. Whether it's planning a date, having a conversation, or working through conflict—do it with your might.

This doesn't mean perfection; it means intention. Give your marriage your best energy, not what's leftover. Pursue your spouse like you're still dating. Work on problems like your marriage depends on it—because it does. Whatever marriage work your hand finds today, don't phone it in. Do it with all your might.

Reflection Question: What marriage task needs your full might today?

DAY 86

"Now the God of patience and consolation grant you to be likeminded one toward another according to Christ Jesus." – Romans 15:5 (KJV)

Being likeminded doesn't mean identical thinking—it means harmonized hearts. Like instruments in an orchestra, you maintain your unique sound while contributing to the same symphony.

God grants this unity, but you must receive it. It comes through patience with differences and consolation in difficulties. When you comfort each other's struggles and wait patiently for growth, minds begin to align.

Seek harmony, not uniformity. Your differences can create beautiful music when surrendered to the same Conductor.

Reflection Question: Where do you need God's help to become more likeminded?

DAY 87

"And if a house be divided against itself, that house cannot stand." – Mark 3:25 (KJV)

Division in marriage rarely happens suddenly. It's small fractures that go unrepaired—unresolved arguments, unspoken hurts, unmet needs. Eventually, the house falls.

Check for cracks in your foundation. Are you presenting a united front to your children? Are you supporting each other publicly? Are you truly on the same team, or have you become polite adversaries?

A house united stands through any storm. Repair the divisions before they become structural.

Reflection Question: What division needs healing in your house today?

DAY 88

"Look not every man on his own things, but every man also on the things of others." – Philippians 2:4 (KJV)

Selfishness is marriage's silent killer. It whispers, "What about my needs? My dreams? My happiness?" But Paul prescribes the antidote: look to your spouse's interests.

This doesn't mean neglecting yourself—notice "also." It means expanding your concern beyond yourself. What does your spouse need? What are they worried about? What brings them joy?

When both partners look out for each other, both get looked after. It's marriage mathematics: give and receive multiplied.

Reflection Question: What interest of your spouse can you prioritize today?

DAY 89

"The righteous shall flourish like the palm tree: he shall grow like a cedar in Lebanon." – Psalm 92:12 (KJV)

Palm trees bend but don't break. Cedars grow slowly but stand strong. Your marriage needs both qualities—flexibility and strength, resilience and deep roots.

Flourishing doesn't mean absence of storms. Palm trees thrive in hurricanes because they bend. Cedars endure centuries because they grow deep before growing tall. Your marriage can flourish through anything with the right foundation. Be patient with your growth. You're not building a paper flower but a mighty tree.

Reflection Question: How is your marriage flourishing despite challenges?

DAY 90

"And God saw every thing that he had made, and, behold, it was very good." – Genesis 1:31 (KJV)

God looked at creation—including marriage—and called it very good. Not perfect, not problem-free, but very good. Can you see your marriage through God's eyes?

Yes, there are struggles. Yes, there's room for growth. But at its core, your marriage is God's very good creation. Two people becoming one, reflecting His image, displaying His love—that's very good. As March ends, celebrate the goodness of what God is creating in your marriage. It's better than you sometimes see.

Reflection Question: What's "very good" about your marriage that you need to acknowledge?

APRIL: RENEWED HOPE

DAY 91

"Sing unto the LORD a new song, and his praise from the end of the earth."
– Isaiah 42:10 (KJV)

April showers bring May flowers, but first comes the rain. Your marriage might be in a rainy season—conflicts, disappointments, or just routine drowning out joy. Time for a new song.

A new song doesn't mean forgetting the old ones. It means adding fresh verses to your love story. Maybe you've been singing the blues lately. Try harmony instead. Praise what's good while working on what's hard.

New songs come from new perspectives. What if your current struggle is actually preparing soil for future growth?

Reflection Question: What new song can you sing over your marriage today?

DAY 92

"For I will restore health unto thee, and I will heal thee of thy wounds, saith the LORD." – Jeremiah 30:17 (KJV)

Some marriages carry wounds—betrayals, harsh words, broken trust. Like untreated injuries, they affect everything. But God promises restoration, and He specializes in marriage healing.

Healing rarely happens instantly. It's daily choosing forgiveness, rebuilding trust one brick at a time, allowing God to do what you can't. That wound that seems unhealable? God says otherwise. Don't rush the healing process, but don't prevent it either. Open your wounds to the Great Physician.

Reflection Question: What wound in your marriage needs God's healing touch?

DAY 93

"But they that wait upon the LORD shall renew their strength; they shall mount up with wings as eagles." – Isaiah 40:31 (KJV)

Marriage exhaustion is real. You're tired of having the same argument, tired of trying without seeing change, tired of being tired. You need renewed strength, not just rest.

Waiting on the Lord isn't passive—it's actively depending on Him rather than your own efforts. It's praying instead of nagging, trusting instead of controlling, believing instead of despairing. Eagles don't flap frantically; they ride wind currents. Let God's strength carry your marriage above the exhaustion.

Reflection Question: Where do you need renewed strength in your marriage?

DAY 94

"Create in me a clean heart, O God; and renew a right spirit within me." –
Psalm 51:10 (KJV)

Before you can fix your marriage, you might need to fix your heart. That bitterness you're nursing? That pride you're protecting? That unforgiveness you're justifying? They're polluting everything.

A clean heart sees your spouse through grace-filled eyes. A right spirit responds with love, not revenge. This isn't about being perfect—it's about being willing to let God clean house.

You can't change your spouse, but you can invite God to change you. Start there.

Reflection Question: What needs cleaning in your heart toward your spouse?

DAY 95

"And he that sat upon the throne said, Behold, I make all things new." –
Revelation 21:5 (KJV)

God's not in the business of patching things up—He makes them new. Your tired marriage? He can renew it. Your broken trust? He can rebuild it. Your lost love? He can resurrect it.

"All things new" includes marriages that feel old, stale, or dying. But you have to let Him work. Stop trying to revive what needs resurrection. Let God make it new instead of trying to make it work.

New is possible, even after years of old patterns.

Reflection Question: What area of your marriage needs God to make new?

DAY 96

"Brethren, I count not myself to have apprehended: but this one thing I do, forgetting those things which are behind, and reaching forth unto those things which are before." – Philippians 3:13 (KJV)

Your marriage's past doesn't have to define its future. Those early mistakes? That season of distance? That major failure? Paul says forget what's behind and reach forward.

This isn't denial—it's decision. Decide that yesterday's failures won't dictate tomorrow's possibilities. Your marriage can be different starting today. But you have to stop rehearsing history and start writing new chapters.

Reach forward together. Your best days can still be ahead.

Reflection Question: What past do you need to forget to reach forward together?

DAY 97

"The flowers appear on the earth; the time of the singing of birds is come." – Song of Solomon 2:12 (KJV)

After every winter comes spring. After every difficult season in marriage comes opportunity for new growth. Look closely— are flowers beginning to appear?

Maybe it's small—a kinder word, a gentle touch, a moment of laughter. These are flowers pushing through frozen ground. Celebrate them. Water them with gratitude. They signal spring's arrival.

Don't miss the small signs of renewal because you're focused on what's still frozen.

Reflection Question: What small flowers of renewal can you see in your marriage?

DAY 98

"This is the day which the LORD hath made; we will rejoice and be glad in it." – Psalm 118:24 (KJV)

Today isn't just another day in your marriage—it's a gift, complete with new mercies and fresh opportunities. Yesterday's argument doesn't have to poison today's potential.

Choose gladness even if you don't feel it. Rejoice in having another day together, another chance to love better, another opportunity to grow. This day will never come again—don't waste it on yesterday's grievances.

Your marriage gets one shot at today. Make it count.

Reflection Question: How can you rejoice in this specific day with your spouse?

DAY 99

"And Jesus said unto them, Because of your unbelief: for verily I say unto you, If ye have faith as a grain of mustard seed, ye shall say unto this mountain, Remove hence to yonder place; and it shall remove." – Matthew 17:20 (KJV)

That mountain in your marriage—the one that seems immovable—only requires mustard-seed faith. Not perfect faith, not enormous faith, just seed-sized faith planted in God's power.

Your mountain might be communication, intimacy, trust, or forgiveness. You've tried pushing it yourself. Now try faith. Speak to it together. Pray over it together. Believe together.

Mountains move slowly sometimes, but they do move when faith is applied.

Reflection Question: What mountain needs mustard-seed faith in your marriage?

DAY 100

"There is therefore now no condemnation to them which are in Christ Jesus." – Romans 8:1 (KJV)

Stop condemning yourself for not being a perfect spouse. Stop condemning your partner for their imperfections. If Christ doesn't condemn, why do you?

Condemnation paralyzes growth. Grace empowers it. When you remove condemnation from your marriage, you create space for transformation. People change in acceptance, not under attack.

Replace condemnation with conviction—one tears down, the other builds up with purpose.

Reflection Question: What condemnation needs to be lifted from your marriage?

DAY 101

"I can do all things through Christ which strengtheneth me." – Philippians 4:13 (KJV)

"All things" includes forgiving again, staying patient, choosing kindness when you're hurt. It includes having that hard conversation, setting that boundary, making that change.

Notice it's "through Christ," not through willpower. Your own strength runs out by Tuesday. Christ's strength is renewable daily. When you can't, He can through you.

Stop saying "I can't" to what your marriage needs. With Christ's strength, you can.

Reflection Question: What "impossible" thing in your marriage needs Christ's strength?

DAY 102

"Let us hold fast the profession of our faith without wavering; (for he is faithful that promised)." – Hebrews 10:23 (KJV)

Your marriage vows were a profession of faith—faith in each other, faith in love, faith in "till death do us part." Hold fast even when waves crash against your commitment.

Wavering happens when you focus on circumstances instead of promises. God is faithful to His promises; be faithful to yours. That covenant you made isn't just between you two—it's a three-way promise with God.

Hold fast. The waves will calm, but only if you don't let go.

Reflection Question: Where do you need to hold fast without wavering?

DAY 103

"For his anger endureth but a moment; in his favour is life: weeping may endure for a night, but joy cometh in the morning." – Psalm 30:5 (KJV)

That fight last night feels like it could end everything. But morning brings perspective. Anger passes, but favor remains. Tears dry, but joy returns.

This is marriage's rhythm—conflict and resolution, tears and laughter, night and morning. Don't make permanent decisions during temporary emotions. Morning is coming with fresh mercy and renewed joy.

Your current weeping has an expiration date. Joy is already on the schedule.

Reflection Question: What temporary pain are you treating as permanent?

DAY 104

"Come unto me, all ye that labour and are heavy laden, and I will give you rest." – Matthew 11:28 (KJV)

Marriage shouldn't feel like hauling bricks uphill every day. If you're exhausted from trying to make it work, Jesus invites you both to rest.

Rest doesn't mean giving up—it means giving over. Hand Him the burden of being perfect spouses. Let Him carry the weight of your expectations. Stop laboring in your own strength.

Sometimes the most productive thing you can do for your marriage is rest in God's grace together.

Reflection Question: What burden do you need to bring to Jesus for rest?

DAY 105

"Therefore if any man be in Christ, he is a new creature: old things are passed away; behold, all things are become new." – 2 Corinthians 5:17 (KJV)

You're not the same person who got married. Neither is your spouse. In Christ, you're both new creatures, constantly being renewed. Stop holding each other to who you used to be.

That mistake they made five years ago? They're not that person anymore. That pattern you struggled with? Old you. God is making you both new daily—let your marriage reflect that renewal.

Give each other permission to grow and change. New creatures need room to become.

Reflection Question: How can you see your spouse as the new creature they're becoming?

DAY 106

"Peace I leave with you, my peace I give unto you: not as the world giveth, give I unto you." – John 14:27 (KJV)

World peace depends on circumstances—everything going right, no conflicts, perfect harmony. Christ's peace exists despite circumstances. Your marriage needs His version.

His peace doesn't mean no disagreements. It means security despite them. It's knowing you're in this together even when you can't agree. It's trusting the foundation while weathering the storm.

Stop seeking circumstantial peace. Receive Christ's peace that surpasses understanding.

Reflection Question: Where does your marriage need Christ's peace rather than world's peace?

DAY 107

"The LORD will perfect that which concerneth me: thy mercy, O LORD, endureth for ever." – Psalm 138:8 (KJV)

God's not finished with your marriage. What concerns you about it concerns Him more. He's perfecting what you can't, finishing what you've started, completing what seems incomplete.

Your part is cooperation, not perfection. Let Him work. Stop interfering with anxiety. His mercy endures through every mistake, every setback, every imperfection.

Trust the process. God finishes what He starts, and He started something beautiful in your union.

Reflection Question: What concerns about your marriage can you trust God to perfect?

DAY 108

"But God, who is rich in mercy, for his great love wherewith he loved us." –
Ephesians 2:4 (KJV)

"But God"—two words that change everything. Your marriage feels broken, BUT GOD. You've run out of patience, BUT GOD. You don't know how to fix this, BUT GOD.

His rich mercy covers your poor attempts. His great love overcomes your small affections. When your love runs dry, His overflows. When your mercy expires, His continues.

Let "But God" become your marriage's turning point.

Reflection Question: What situation needs a "But God" intervention?

DAY 109

"Now faith is the substance of things hoped for, the evidence of things not
seen." – Hebrews 11:1 (KJV)

Faith in marriage means believing in what you're building even when you can't see it yet. It's trusting the seeds you're planting will grow. It's knowing today's investment pays tomorrow's dividends.

You might not see improvement yet, but faith says it's coming. You might not feel different yet, but faith trusts transformation is happening. Faith sees your marriage not as it is, but as it's becoming.

Keep believing. What you're hoping for has substance, even if invisible.

Reflection Question: What unseen hope needs your faith today?

DAY 110

"Delight thyself also in the LORD; and he shall give thee the desires of thine heart." – Psalm 37:4 (KJV)

When you delight in God together, your desires align—with His will and with each other. You stop wanting opposite things and start craving the same things: peace, purpose, presence.

Delighting in the Lord isn't a transaction for getting what you want. It's transformation that changes what you want. Your heart's desires shift from selfish to sacred, from temporary to eternal.

Make delighting in God a couple's pursuit. Watch your desires harmonize.

Reflection Question: How can you delight in the Lord together today?

DAY 111

"Be still, and know that I am God." – Psalm 46:10 (KJV)

Your marriage might need less fixing and more stillness. Stop frantically trying to solve everything. Be still together. Remember who's really in control.

Stillness isn't inactivity—it's intentional rest in God's sovereignty. It's choosing trust over hysteria, peace over panic. In stillness, you hear what chaos drowns out: God's still small voice.

Schedule stillness in your marriage. Turn off the noise. Be quiet together. Know He is God.

Reflection Question: Where does your marriage need stillness instead of striving?

DAY 112

"My soul, wait thou only upon God; for my expectation is from him." –
Psalm 62:5 (KJV)

Your spouse can't meet all your expectations—they weren't designed to. Only God can fully satisfy your soul's deepest needs. When you expect from God what only He can give, your spouse is freed from impossible pressure.

This doesn't lower marriage expectations—it properly places them. Expect companionship from your spouse, completion from God. Expect partnership from your spouse, perfection from God.

Adjust your expectations' source. It changes everything.

Reflection Question: What expectation do you need to shift from your spouse to God?

DAY 113

"And let the peace of God rule in your hearts, to the which also ye are called in one body." – *Colossians 3:15 (KJV)*

Let peace be the referee in your marriage. When conflict arises, ask: "What would peace choose?" When decisions loom, consider: "Which option leads to peace?"

You're called to peace in one body—your marriage body. Not separate peace, but shared peace. When one lacks peace, both should be concerned. When peace rules, both win.

Make peace your marriage's decision-maker.

Reflection Question: What decision needs peace to rule over?

DAY 114

"I will praise thee; for I am fearfully and wonderfully made." – Psalm 139:14 (KJV)

Your spouse is God's masterpiece—fearfully and wonderfully made. Yes, even with their quirks. Especially with their uniqueness. God doesn't make mistakes, and He made them specifically for you.

When you criticize your spouse's core design, you're critiquing the Creator. Instead, praise God for how He crafted them. Celebrate their unique wiring instead of trying to rewire them.

Your spouse is not a project to fix but a gift to treasure.

Reflection Question: What wonderful aspect of your spouse's design can you praise God for?

DAY 115

"Casting down imaginations, and every high thing that exalteth itself against the knowledge of God, and bringing into captivity every thought." – 2 Corinthians 10:5 (KJV)

Those imaginary arguments you have with your spouse in your head? Cast them down. Those assumptions about their motives? Take them captive. Your thought life shapes your marriage life.

Don't let imagination write stories about your spouse's intentions. Don't build cases in your mind. Capture those thoughts before they become beliefs, beliefs before they become actions. Guard your mind about your marriage. What you think determines what you see.

Reflection Question: What imagination about your spouse needs casting down?

DAY 116

"I have learned, in whatsoever state I am, therewith to be content." –
Philippians 4:11 (KJV)

Contentment in marriage isn't settling for less—it's recognizing you have enough. Enough love, even if expressed differently than you prefer. Enough blessing, even if packaged unexpectedly.

Paul learned contentment; it wasn't natural. You can learn it too. Stop comparing your marriage to others. Stop waiting for perfection to be satisfied. Learn contentment in this season, with this person, in this reality. Contentment breeds gratitude. Gratitude breeds joy. Joy strengthens marriages.

Reflection Question: Where do you need to learn contentment in your marriage?

DAY 117

"The Lord GOD hath given me the tongue of the learned, that I should know how to speak a word in season to him that is weary." – Isaiah 50:4
(KJV)

Your spouse needs timely words—encouragement when discouraged, comfort when grieving, celebration when succeeding. Learn the seasons of their soul and speak accordingly.

A word in season can revive a weary spouse. But it requires paying attention, learning their rhythms, recognizing their needs. Sometimes they need challenge; sometimes they need comfort. Wisdom knows the difference. Be a student of your spouse. Learn to speak seasonal words.

Reflection Question: What word in season does your weary spouse need?

DAY 118

"Hope deferred maketh the heart sick: but when the desire cometh, it is a tree of life." – Proverbs 13:12 (KJV)

Maybe you've been hoping for change, for breakthrough, for restoration—and waiting hurts. Deferred hope does make hearts sick. But don't give up. When desire comes, it brings life.

That improvement you're hoping for, that healing you're praying for, that breakthrough you're believing for—it's not just possible, it's promised to bring life when it arrives. The waiting is hard, but the fulfillment is worth it. Keep hoping. Trees of life are growing from today's seeds of hope.

Reflection Question: What deferred hope needs renewed faith in your marriage?

DAY 119

"For where two or three are gathered together in my name, there am I in the midst of them." – Matthew 18:20 (KJV)

You and your spouse are the minimum required for God's presence. When you gather in His name—to pray, to worship, to seek Him—He shows up. Your marriage is a congregation of two, and God attends every service.

Make your marriage a gathering place for God's presence. Invite Him into conversations, decisions, and daily life. He's not an intruder but an invited guest who brings gifts.

Gather together in His name. Watch Him show up in the midst.

Reflection Question: How can you gather in God's name as a couple today?

DAY 120

"Behold, how good and how pleasant it is for brethren to dwell together in unity!" – Psalm 133:1 (KJV)

Unity doesn't mean uniformity. You can be united while being different. Unity means same team, same goals, same commitment—not same personality, same opinions, same approaches.

Unity is both good (functionally beneficial) and pleasant (emotionally satisfying). It makes marriage work better and feel better. But unity requires intention—choosing connection over correction, harmony over being right.

As April ends, celebrate any unity you've built. It's good and pleasant, and God loves it.

Reflection Question: Where has your marriage grown in unity this month?

MAY: FLOURISHING TOGETHER

DAY 121

"He hath made every thing beautiful in his time." – Ecclesiastes 3:11 (KJV)

May brings flowers that were just seeds in March. Your marriage works the same way—what looks unfinished today is still becoming beautiful. God's not rushed. He's making everything beautiful in its time, including your relationship.

That conversation you've been avoiding might bloom into deeper understanding. The patience you're practicing now could flower into unshakeable trust later. Even your struggles are part of the beauty-making process, like rain that seems inconvenient but makes everything grow.

Think about how different you both were five years ago. See the beauty that time has already created? There's more coming. God's still working, still making things beautiful. Your marriage is right on schedule—His schedule.

Trust the timing. What feels late to you might be perfectly punctual to God.

Reflection Question: What area of your marriage is God making beautiful in His time?

DAY 122

"She is more precious than rubies: and all the things thou canst desire are not to be compared unto her." – Proverbs 31:10 (KJV)

Your spouse isn't competing with your hobbies, career, or dreams—they're in a category of their own. Rubies are valuable, but they can't laugh at your jokes, hold you in hard times, or build a life with you. Too often, we polish our careers while letting our marriages tarnish. Look at your spouse today—beyond the morning hair and coffee breath—and see the treasure you've been given. They're not perfect (rubies have flaws too), but they're priceless. Stop window shopping for what you think you're missing and start treasuring what you already have.

Reflection Question: How can you show your spouse they're your greatest treasure today?

DAY 123

"For this cause shall a man leave father and mother, and shall cleave to his wife, and they twain shall be one flesh." – Mark 10:7-8 (KJV)

Leaving isn't just physical distance—it's emotional and spiritual independence. Some couples live far from family but still filter decisions through "What will mom think?" or let invisible advisors join every conflict. Cleaving means prioritizing your spouse's opinion over your parents' and their needs over old preferences. Honor your parents without being controlled by them. Your marriage needs space to grow its own roots, free from extended family drama. You're building something new, not recreating what you came from. Your first loyalty is to each other now. Act like it.

Reflection Question: Where do you need to "leave" more fully to "cleave" better?

DAY 124

"Let thy fountain be blessed: and rejoice with the wife of thy youth." –
Proverbs 5:18 (KJV)

Remember when everything about your spouse fascinated
you—their stories, dreams, even how they held their coffee
cup? That rejoicing shouldn't be past tense. The person you
fell for is still there, now with more layers—like a favorite song
revealing new notes over time. Celebrate who they are today,
not just who they were. Yes, you've both changed, and reality
has replaced some romance, but there's still so much to rejoice
in. Notice their persistence, silly humor, or faithful presence.
Rejoice as you did in youth, but with the depth and richness
that only time can bring.

Reflection Question: What can you rejoice about in your spouse
today?

DAY 125

"Likewise, ye husbands, dwell with them according to knowledge." – 1 Peter
3:7 (KJV)

Living with your spouse "according to knowledge" means being a lifelong student of them. What stressed them yesterday
might not today, and what brought joy last year might not
now. Marriage thrives when both spouses keep learning—
exploring current dreams, fears, and desires. Don't rely on old
information; your spouse isn't the same person you married—
hopefully, they're better. Stay curious and keep discovering
who they are becoming.

Reflection Question: What new thing do you need to learn
about your spouse?

DAY 126

"It is better to dwell in a corner of the housetop, than with a brawling woman in a wide house." – Proverbs 21:9 (KJV)

This isn't just about wives—anyone can make home miserable with constant conflict. A mansion feels like a prison with arguments, while a tiny apartment feels like paradise with peace. Are you making your home a refuge or a battlefield? That "discussion" you keep having—does it build or brawl? Sometimes being right costs more than being wrong. Hearts grow narrow with constant conflict. Choose your battles—or better yet, choose peace. Make home a place to breathe, not brace for impact. A peaceful corner beats a contentious castle every time.

Reflection Question: What conflict can you let go to create more peace at home?

DAY 127

"Wherefore they are no more twain, but one flesh. What therefore God hath joined together, let not man put asunder." – Matthew 19:6 (KJV)

You're not roommates with rings—you're one flesh, divinely joined. Your spouse's pain is yours, their victories too. This union isn't just legal; it's spiritual. "Let not man put asunder" includes you—don't threaten divorce, live separate lives, or let others wedge between you, whether kids, parents, or friends. God joined you; your job is to protect that bond. Every choice either strengthens or weakens it. Choose to strengthen it.

Reflection Question: What threatens to put asunder what God has joined in your marriage?

DAY 128

"House and riches are the inheritance of fathers: and a prudent wife is from the LORD." – Proverbs 19:14 (KJV)

You might inherit money or property, but a wise spouse? That's a gift straight from God. No inheritance compares to a partner who makes prudent choices, speaks wisely, and builds rather than breaks. This applies to both spouses—wisdom in marriage is God's provision. When your spouse shows prudence, even when you don't, that's God protecting you through them. You might not always appreciate their wisdom—especially when it conflicts with what you want—but it's a gift worth thanking Him for.

Reflection Question: What wisdom has God provided through your spouse?

DAY 129

"Neither do men put new wine into old bottles: else the bottles break, and the wine runneth out." – Matthew 9:17 (KJV)

Your marriage can't grow if you're using old patterns for new seasons. What worked as newlyweds might not work with teenagers, and year-one communication may not fit year ten. New seasons demand new approaches. Still fighting like five years ago? Time for new wineskins. Still treating each other based on old wounds? Those bottles need replacing. God wants to pour new wine into your marriage, but you need containers that can hold it. Don't cling to "how we've always done it" and miss what God wants to do now. Embrace growth and let Him renew your relationship.

Reflection Question: What old pattern needs replacing with something new?

DAY 130

"Her husband is known in the gates, when he sitteth among the elders of the land." – Proverbs 31:23 (KJV)

How you speak about your spouse in public matters. Are you building their reputation or tearing it down? That "harmless" complaint to friends, that eye roll when they're talking—it all adds up. Your spouse's reputation is partly in your hands. When you honor them publicly, you're building something beautiful. When you criticize them to others, you're demolishing what God is constructing. Be your spouse's biggest promoter, not their harshest critic. Make your spouse "known in the gates" for good reasons. Brag about their strengths more than you broadcast their weaknesses.

Reflection Question: How can you enhance your spouse's reputation today?

DAY 131

"Be ye angry, and sin not: let not the sun go down upon your wrath." – Ephesians 4:26 (KJV)

Anger happens in marriage—you're two different people with different perspectives. But anger becomes sin when it festers, when it seeks revenge, when it builds walls instead of bridges. That rule about not letting the sun go down on wrath? It's not about forced apologies at 11:59 PM. It's about not letting anger ferment into bitterness. Sometimes you go to bed upset but committed to resolution. Sometimes you need sleep before sense returns. Feel your anger, but don't feed it. Express it without exploding. Resolve it without rushing. The sun sets daily; let your anger set too.

Reflection Question: What anger needs to be resolved before it becomes sin?

DAY 132

"Through wisdom is an house builded; and by understanding it is established." – Proverbs 24:3 (KJV)

You're building more than a household—you're building a legacy. Every decision is a brick, every conversation adds structure. Wisdom provides the blueprints; understanding lays the foundation. But building takes time. You don't frame a house in a day or establish understanding in a week. Every wise choice strengthens your structure, and every moment of understanding reinforces your foundation. Some days you're building; some days you're maintaining. Both are essential. Keep building wisely and with understanding—your house is becoming exactly what you're shaping it to be.

Reflection Question: What aspect of your marriage house needs wisdom or understanding today?

DAY 133

"And Adam said, This is now bone of my bones, and flesh of my flesh." – Genesis 2:23 (KJV)

Adam's first words about Eve weren't critique but celebration: "This is now!"—excitement, recognition, gratitude. When did you last feel that about your spouse? They're still bone of your bones, flesh of your flesh. Unity hasn't diminished just because novelty has. Beneath the familiar exterior is the person who made your heart race, chose you above all others, and became one with you. Rediscover the "This is now!" in your marriage—not by comparing to others, but by recognizing the gift you have.

Reflection Question: What makes you say "This is now!" about your spouse today?

DAY 134

"Live joyfully with the wife whom thou lovest all the days of the life of thy vanity." – Ecclesiastes 9:9 (KJV)

Life is short—Solomon calls it vanity, like morning mist that disappears. Don't waste these evaporating days in misery with the person you chose. Live joyfully, not just dutifully. Joy in marriage isn't about perfect circumstances but purposeful choice. Dance in the kitchen even with dishes in the sink. Laugh at the chaos instead of just managing it. Create moments of joy between responsibilities. Your days together are numbered—not to create fear but urgency. Why waste them in unhappiness? Choose joy while you have days to choose.

Reflection Question: How can you live more joyfully with your spouse today?

DAY 135

"A virtuous woman is a crown to her husband: but she that maketh ashamed is as rottenness in his bones." – Proverbs 12:4 (KJV)

Being a crown to your spouse means adding honor, not weight. Both husbands and wives can be crowns—visible symbols of blessing, honor, and favor. Or you can be rottenness, decay from within. How do you affect your spouse? Do they stand taller because of your support or shrink from your criticism? Do you crown them with encouragement or crush them with contempt? Choose to be a crown. Speak words that honor. Take actions that elevate. Make your spouse feel like royalty, not a peasant.

Reflection Question: How can you be more of a crown to your spouse?

DAY 136

"Let the word of Christ dwell in you richly in all wisdom; teaching and admonishing one another in psalms and hymns and spiritual songs." –
Colossians 3:16 (KJV)

When Christ's word dwells in your marriage richly, it changes how you communicate. Criticism becomes constructive. Arguments turn into discussions. Even correction comes wrapped in love. Music changes atmosphere. Try literally singing together—in the car, during chores, in worship. It's hard to stay angry when you're harmonizing. Shared songs create shared memories, shared joy, shared connection. Let God's word be your marriage's soundtrack. Quote scripture to encourage, not condemn. Sing truth over each other. Make melody in your marriage.

Reflection Question: How can Christ's word dwell more richly in your marriage?

DAY 137

"Give, and it shall be given unto you; good measure, pressed down, and shaken together, and running over." – Luke 6:38 (KJV)

Marriage math seems backwards: give more, receive more. But it works. Give patience, receive peace. Give forgiveness, receive freedom. Give love, receive loyalty. The measure you use gets used on you. Stop keeping score of who gave last. Start giving like you have unlimited resources—because through Christ, you do. Don't give to get; give to bless. But watch how blessings boomerang back. Be generous with grace, lavish with love, abundant in affection. Your marriage can't out-give God.

Reflection Question: What can you give generously to your spouse today?

DAY 138

"The aged women likewise, that they be in behaviour as becometh holiness, not false accusers, not given to much wine, teachers of good things; That they may teach the young women to be sober, to love their husbands." –
Titus 2:3-4 (KJV)

Loving your spouse is learned behavior. It's both natural and nurtured, instinctive and instructed. Who's teaching you how to love better? What examples are you following? Find couples who've walked this road longer. Learn from their victories and mistakes. But be careful who you take advice from—not everyone who's been married long has been married well. Also, become teachers yourselves. Some couple is watching you, learning from your love. Make it worth watching.

Reflection Question: Who can teach you to love your spouse better?

DAY 139

"Let another man praise thee, and not thine own mouth; a stranger, and not thine own lips." – Proverbs 27:2 (KJV)

Your spouse needs others to hear how amazing they are—from you. Not self-promotion, but spouse-promotion. Share their victories, growth, and greatness. Be their publicist, not their critic. This creates a beautiful cycle: your praise reminds you of their value, earns them respect from others, and deepens their trust when they hear it. Stop advertising their faults. Start highlighting their features. Let the praise about them come from your lips, not their own.

Reflection Question: Who needs to hear something praiseworthy about your spouse?

DAY 140

"Therefore shall a man leave his father and his mother, and shall cleave unto his wife: and they shall be one flesh." – Genesis 2:24 (KJV)

Becoming one flesh is a process, not just a wedding night event. Every day you're either growing together or apart. Unity requires intention—choosing to intertwine lives, not just share addresses.

One flesh means their pain hurts you, their joy delights you. It's deeper than joint bank accounts; it's joined souls. You're creating something entirely new—not you, not them, but us.

Keep cleaving. It's an active verb, ongoing action. Every day, choose to hold tighter, grow closer, become more unified.

Reflection Question: Where do you need to cleave more closely?

DAY 141

"By love serve one another." – Galatians 5:13 (KJV)

Service in marriage shouldn't feel like servitude. When love motivates service, it transforms from obligation to opportunity. Making their coffee becomes a love letter. Folding their laundry becomes a prayer.

Notice it's mutual—"one another." Not one serving while the other sits. Both serving, both receiving, both blessed. Marriage is a dance of service where both partners take turns leading and following.

Serve from love, not for points. Do it because you get to, not because you have to.

Reflection Question: How can love motivate your service today?

DAY 142

"As for me and my house, we will serve the LORD." – Joshua 24:15 (KJV)

Joshua didn't say "I'll serve the Lord and hope my family follows." He declared their collective commitment. Your marriage needs that same unified declaration—we together, not just parallel individual commitments. Serving the Lord as a couple multiplies impact. Your unified devotion teaches children, influences friends, impacts community. When you both row in God's direction, you move faster and farther.

Make this declaration for your house. Decide together, serve together, stand together.

Reflection Question: How can you better serve the Lord together?

DAY 143

"Who can find a virtuous woman? for her price is far above rubies... Her husband is known in the gates, when he sitteth among the elders of the land." – Proverbs 31:10,23 (KJV)

The Proverbs 31 woman's virtue elevated her husband's position. Your virtue (both husbands and wives) affects your spouse's life. Your character becomes their reputation. Your integrity protects their honor.

This isn't pressure; it's privilege. You have the power to lift your spouse higher through your own growth. When you become better, they benefit. Your virtue is a gift you give your marriage.

Pursue virtue not just for yourself but for your spouse's sake. Your growth is their gain.

Reflection Question: How does your virtue benefit your spouse?

DAY 144

"And they were both naked, the man and his wife, and were not ashamed."
– Genesis 2:25 (KJV)

Nakedness in marriage goes beyond physical—it's emotional and spiritual transparency. No hiding, no pretending, no performing. Just two people fully known and fully accepted.

Shame builds walls where God intended openness. Past wounds create cover-ups. Fear fashions masks. But real intimacy requires the vulnerability of Eden—seeing and being seen without shame. Work toward this transparency. Share the things you hide. Risk being known. The intimacy on the other side of vulnerability is worth the courage it takes.

Reflection Question: Where does shame prevent transparency in your marriage?

DAY 145

"Let us therefore follow after the things which make for peace, and things wherewith one may edify another." – Romans 14:19 (KJV)

Every choice in marriage either builds peace or breaks it. That tone of voice, that facial expression, that word choice—they're either edifying or eroding.

Following after peace means actively pursuing it, not just avoiding conflict. It's choosing calming words over cutting ones. It's building your spouse up when the world tears them down.

Make peace and edification your marriage priorities. Before speaking, ask: "Will this build peace or break it?"

Reflection Question: What can you do today that makes for peace?

DAY 146

"Let him kiss me with the kisses of his mouth: for thy love is better than wine." – Song of Solomon 1:2 (KJV)

Romance isn't juvenile; it's biblical. Solomon's song celebrates physical affection, emotional connection, and romantic love. Your marriage needs all three, not just functional coexistence.

When did you last kiss with intention, not just habit? When did affection last lead somewhere besides duty? Love should intoxicate more than wine—bringing joy, warmth, and celebration. Resurrect romance. Not Hollywood fantasy but real affection. Kiss longer. Hold hands purposefully. Remember that love is meant to be enjoyed, not just endured.

Reflection Question: How can you revive romance in practical ways today?

DAY 147

"Many daughters have done virtuously, but thou excellest them all." – Proverbs 31:29 (KJV)

Your spouse needs to know they excel in your eyes. Not in comparison to others, but in your personal rankings, they're number one. They need to hear they're your favorite, your choice, your prize.

"Many have done well, but you excel them all." Say it. Mean it. Repeat it. In a world of endless options and comparisons, your spouse needs to know they're not in competition—they've already won.

Stop critiquing and start celebrating. Your spouse is excellent. Tell them.

Reflection Question: How does your spouse excel above all others in your eyes?

DAY 148

"For the husband is the head of the wife, even as Christ is the head of the church: and he is the saviour of the body." – Ephesians 5:23 (KJV)

Headship isn't about dominance but responsibility. Christ's headship meant sacrifice, service, and saving. That's the model—leadership that serves, authority that sacrifices, position that protects.

Both spouses lead in different areas. Both serve. Both sacrifice. The goal isn't hierarchy but harmony, not power but partnership. When both follow Christ's example, everyone wins.

Lead by serving. Follow by supporting. Make your marriage a mutual submission to love.

Reflection Question: How can you better serve through your role in marriage?

DAY 149

"Drink waters out of thine own cistern, and running waters out of thine own well." – Proverbs 5:15 (KJV)

Satisfaction is found at home, not in foreign wells. That grass that looks greener? It's often artificial turf. Your own cistern—your spouse—contains all the refreshment you need.

Stop looking elsewhere for what you already have. That attention you crave? Your spouse can provide it. That excitement you miss? It's available at home. But you have to drink from your own well, not window shop at others.

Cultivate satisfaction with what you have. Your well runs deeper than you think.

Reflection Question: What satisfaction do you need to find in your own marriage?

DAY 150

"So ought men to love their wives as their own bodies. He that loveth his wife loveth himself." – Ephesians 5:28 (KJV)

Loving your spouse is self-care at its finest. When you build them up, you rise too. When you tear them down, you're demolishing your own house. You're one flesh—what affects them affects you.

This changes everything. Their happiness becomes your happiness. Their hurt becomes your hurt. You can't wound them without bleeding yourself. You can't bless them without being blessed.

Love your spouse like you love yourself—with care, protection, and provision. It's the smartest selfish thing you can do.

Reflection Question: How is loving your spouse actually loving yourself?

DAY 151

"Let thy garments be always white; and let thy head lack no ointment." – Ecclesiastes 9:8 (KJV)

Keep making effort in your marriage. White garments and anointed heads symbolize celebration, intention, and care. Don't let marriage become sweatpants and yesterday's hair. Stay celebration-ready.

This isn't about vanity but value. When you make effort for your spouse—dressing nicely, staying healthy, maintaining attraction—you're saying they're worth it. You're still trying to win someone you've already won.

Reflection Question: What effort can you make to show your spouse they're still worth pursuing?

June: Summer of Love

Day 152

"My beloved spake, and said unto me, Rise up, my love, my fair one, and come away." – Song of Solomon 2:10 (KJV)

Summer calls for adventure, and your marriage needs some. When did you last "come away" together? Not just physically but mentally—away from routine, responsibility, and roles. Just two people who chose each other, rediscovering why.

Adventure doesn't require airplane tickets. It might be trying that new restaurant, taking a different route home, or staying up late talking like teenagers. It's breaking patterns that have become prisons.

Your beloved is calling: "Rise up and come away." Answer the invitation. Create space for spontaneity. Let summer remind you that marriage should include joy, not just duty.

Reflection Question: What adventure can you plan with your spouse this summer?

DAY 153

"Favour is deceitful, and beauty is vain: but a woman that feareth the LORD, she shall be praised." – Proverbs 31:30 (KJV)

Physical beauty fades—that's biology. But spiritual beauty grows. Early in marriage, you may have focused on outward attraction. Now you have the privilege of discovering inner beauty—character that deepens with time. Watch your spouse's faith, their trust in God through trials, their perseverance through problems. That's lasting beauty, worth celebrating. Both husbands and wives grow more beautiful as they grow closer to God. Celebrate the beauty time can't steal. Your spouse is becoming more praiseworthy, not less.

Reflection Question: What inner beauty in your spouse deserves praise?

DAY 154

"Thou hast ravished my heart, my sister, my spouse; thou hast ravished my heart with one of thine eyes." – Song of Solomon 4:9 (KJV)

Can your spouse still ravish your heart with a glance? That flutter isn't just for newlyweds. Long-married couples can still feel butterflies—they just have to pay attention.

Notice the small things that made you fall in love. The way they concentrate. Their laugh. How they interact with children. Let your heart be ravished again by familiar things seen with fresh eyes.

Romance doesn't die with time; neglect kills it. Revive your ability to be ravished. Your spouse still has the power to captivate you.

Reflection Question: What about your spouse can still ravish your heart?

DAY 155

"I will betroth thee unto me for ever; yea, I will betroth thee unto me in righteousness." – Hosea 2:19 (KJV)

Betrothal was serious business—legally binding, socially recognized, spiritually significant. Your marriage vows weren't just words but eternal betrothal. "For ever" means something when God's involved.

This permanence brings freedom. You don't have to audition daily. You're not on probation. You're betrothed—chosen, committed, secure. That security should create peace, not complacency.

Live like you're betrothed for ever. Stop treating marriage like a trial period. Settle into the security of permanent choice.

Reflection Question: How does eternal betrothal change how you view your marriage?

DAY 156

"Marriage is honourable in all, and the bed undefiled." – Hebrews 13:4 (KJV)

God created marriage and called it honorable—all of it. The friendship, partnership, and yes, the physical intimacy. What God designed, shame shouldn't diminish. Your marriage bed is blessed, not just biological.

Honor requires intention. Protect your marriage from comparison, pornography, and emotional affairs. Keep the bed undefiled by maintaining exclusive intimacy—emotional and physical. What happens in your marriage is sacred.

Celebrate the honor of marriage. It's not society's throwaway relationship but God's honored institution.

Reflection Question: How can you better honor the sacredness of your marriage?

DAY 157

"How fair and how pleasant art thou, O love, for delights!" – Song of Solomon 7:6 (KJV)

Your spouse was designed for delights—yours specifically. They're not just a responsibility or roommate but a source of pleasure, joy, and satisfaction. When did you last delighted in them rather than just dealt with them?

Find the delights. Maybe it's their humor, their wisdom, their presence. Maybe it's how they make coffee or tell stories. God gave you this person for delight, not just duty.

Stop focusing on what irritates and start noticing what delights. They're there, waiting to be enjoyed.

Reflection Question: What delights about your spouse have you been overlooking?

DAY 158

"Nevertheless, to avoid fornication, let every man have his own wife, and let every woman have her own husband." – 1 Corinthians 7:2 (KJV)

"His own wife," "her own husband"—exclusive possession, mutual belonging. In a world of options, you've chosen exclusivity. That's not limitation; it's liberation. You don't have to keep auditioning or competing.

This exclusivity protects and provides. It protects from temptation while providing intimacy. You have someone who's yours alone, and you're theirs alone. That's rare and precious.

Guard your exclusivity. Celebrate your mutual belonging. You're each other's "own"—what a gift.

Reflection Question: How can you celebrate the exclusivity of belonging to each other?

DAY 159

"I am my beloved's, and my beloved is mine." – Song of Solomon 6:3 (KJV)

Mutual possession—you're not losing yourself but finding yourself in belonging. "I am my beloved's" speaks to complete giving. "My beloved is mine" celebrates complete receiving. Both are necessary.

This isn't possessiveness but partnership. You belong to each other in ways you belong to no one else. That belonging brings responsibility and privilege, burden and blessing.

Embrace the belonging. Stop holding back parts of yourself. Give completely, receive fully.

Reflection Question: What part of yourself are you withholding from belonging?

DAY 160

"And they shall be one flesh." – Genesis 2:24 (KJV)

One flesh is mystery and miracle. Two separate histories becoming one future. Two different perspectives creating one vision. It's not mathematical—one plus one somehow equals one.

This unity is progressive. You're more one flesh now than on your wedding day. Every shared experience, every overcome obstacle, every moment of intimacy weaves you tighter together.

Celebrate the mystery. You're becoming something neither could be alone—one flesh, unified and unique.

Reflection Question: How have you become more "one flesh" this year?

DAY 161

"Wives, submit yourselves unto your own husbands, as unto the Lord." –
Ephesians 5:22 (KJV)

Submission isn't about inferiority but order. Like dancers, someone leads, someone follows, both are essential. This verse gets misused, but properly understood, it's about mutual respect and willing cooperation.

Both spouses submit—to God first, then to each other's strengths. You submit to their wisdom in their areas of expertise. They submit to yours in yours. It's choreographed cooperation, not domination. Find the dance of mutual submission. Lead where you're strong, follow where they're stronger.

Reflection Question: Where can mutual submission strengthen your marriage?

DAY 162

"Whoso loveth instruction loveth knowledge: but he that hateth reproof is brutish." – Proverbs 12:1 (KJV)

Your spouse's feedback is a gift, even when it stings. They see blind spots you can't. When they offer instruction or correction, they're investing in your growth, not attacking your character.

Loving instruction means welcoming your spouse's insights. "You always do that" might hurt, but it might also be helpful. "Can I suggest something?" shouldn't trigger defense but invite discussion.

Don't be brutish—stubborn and unteachable. Love knowledge enough to receive it from your closest observer.

Reflection Question: What instruction from your spouse do you need to receive?

DAY 163

"Let her be as the loving hind and pleasant roe; let her breasts satisfy thee at all times; and be thou ravished always with her love." – Proverbs 5:19 (KJV)

God isn't prudish about married love—He celebrates it, encourages it, even commands satisfaction in it. Your spouse should ravish you—not just physically, but emotionally, continually, and exclusively. Words like "always" and "at all times" in Scripture suggest consistency, not just rare moments. Daily ravishing, regular satisfaction, and continual choosing are part of God's design. Don't let routine make the idea of ravishing seem ridiculous. Be ravished. Stay satisfied. Keep choosing to be intoxicated by your spouse's love.

Reflection Question: How can you cultivate being "ravished always" in your marriage?

DAY 164

"I have compared thee, O my love, to a company of horses in Pharaoh's chariots." – Song of Solomon 1:9 (KJV)

Strange compliment? Not in Solomon's day. Pharaoh's horses were the finest—strong, beautiful, valuable, and trusted. Your spouse needs to know they're your premium choice, not your settling option. Comparison to others destroys; comparison to ideals disappoints. But celebrating your spouse as finest in your eyes? That builds. They need to know they're your Pharaoh's horses—the best of the best to you. Find new ways to say "You're amazing." Make comparisons that celebrate rather than criticize.

Reflection Question: What unique compliment can you give your spouse?

DAY 165

"Hearken, O daughter, and consider, and incline thine ear; forget also thine own people, and thy father's house." – Psalm 45:10 (KJV)

Starting fresh sometimes means forgetting what's familiar. Your marriage can't thrive if you're constantly comparing it to your parents' or trying to recreate your childhood home. You're building something new.

Forgetting doesn't mean dishonoring but differentiating. Your marriage gets to have its own culture, traditions, and patterns. Stop trying to duplicate and start creating something unique.

Incline your ear to your spouse, not echoes from the past. Build your own house.

Reflection Question: What pattern from the past needs forgetting for your future?

DAY 166

"Set me as a seal upon thine heart." – Song of Solomon 8:6 (KJV)

Seals marked ownership and authenticity. Your spouse wants to be sealed on your heart—permanently marked as yours, impossible to counterfeit, clearly claimed.

This sealing is mutual. You're marked by marriage in ways visible and invisible. Your decisions now consider another. Your plans include them. Your heart bears their seal.

Wear the seal proudly. Let everyone know your heart is taken, marked, sealed.

Reflection Question: How can you show your spouse they're sealed upon your heart?

DAY 167

"Hatred stirreth up strifes: but love covereth all sins." – Proverbs 10:12 (KJV)

Every marriage has sins that need covering—not hiding but healing through love. That thing they did? Love can cover it. That pattern that frustrates? Love provides a blanket.

Covering isn't ignoring but choosing love over litigation. It's addressing issues from love's perspective, not hate's hunger for justice. When love covers, healing happens underneath.

Be generous with your covering. Love covers all sins, not just convenient ones.

Reflection Question: What sin needs love's covering in your marriage today?

DAY 168

"Therefore take no thought for the morrow: for the morrow shall take thought for the things of itself." – Matthew 6:34 (KJV)

Anxiety about tomorrow steals joy from today. That future worry you're carrying? It's robbing present peace. Your marriage has enough beauty today without borrowing tomorrow's troubles.

This doesn't mean don't plan but don't panic. Tomorrow's problems will come with tomorrow's grace. Today's grace is for today's challenges. Stop spending future resources on current moments.

Be present in your marriage. Tomorrow will handle itself; today needs your attention.

Reflection Question: What tomorrow-worry is stealing from your today?

DAY 169

"Where no wood is, there the fire goeth out: so where there is no talebearer, the strife ceaseth." – Proverbs 26:20 (KJV)

Stop adding wood to marriage fires. That complaint to your mom? Wood. That venting session with friends? More wood. Every time you broadcast your spouse's faults, you're fueling strife.

Fires die without fuel. Stop feeding them with gossip, complaints, and comparisons. Instead of adding wood, add water. Speak well of your spouse to others. Share their victories, not just their failures.

Let strife cease by cutting off its fuel supply.

Reflection Question: What wood do you need to stop adding to marriage fires?

DAY 170

"She will do him good and not evil all the days of her life." – Proverbs 31:12 (KJV)

Consistency matters. Not perfection, but persistent choosing of good over evil, building over breaking, helping over hurting. This applies to both spouses—doing good all the days, not just good days. Good looks like patience on hard days, kindness when tired, support when you disagree. It's choosing their benefit even when it costs you. Evil is subtle—withholding affection, broadcasting faults, keeping score. Choose good today, tomorrow, all the days. Consistency creates security.

Reflection Question: How can you consistently do good to your spouse?

DAY 171

"Let not mercy and truth forsake thee: bind them about thy neck; write them upon the table of thine heart." – Proverbs 3:3 (KJV)

Your marriage needs both mercy and truth—not one or the other. Truth without mercy crushes. Mercy without truth enables. Together, they transform. Bind them around your neck like jewelry you never remove. Write them on your heart where they influence every beat. When you speak truth, wrap it in mercy. When you extend mercy, include truth. Don't let either forsake your marriage. You need both, always, together.

Reflection Question: Does your marriage need more mercy or more truth right now?

DAY 172

"Thy wife shall be as a fruitful vine by the sides of thine house." – Psalm 128:3 (KJV)

Vines need support to be fruitful. Your spouse needs your structure, encouragement, and stability to flourish. You're not just married to them; you're their trellis, their support system, their growth partner.

Fruitfulness in marriage isn't just about children but about what you produce together—love, joy, peace, impact. When you support each other's growth, you both become more fruitful.

Be the support your spouse needs to flourish. Watch what grows.

Reflection Question: How can you better support your spouse's fruitfulness?

DAY 173

"And the rib, which the LORD God had taken from man, made he a woman, and brought her unto the man." – Genesis 2:22 (KJV)

God brought Eve to Adam—divine matchmaking at its finest. Your spouse was brought to you, not by accident but by providence. Even if you met online or at a bar, God was involved in the bringing.

This changes everything. They're not random but providential. Your meeting wasn't chance but choreographed. God brought you together for purposes beyond your understanding.

Trust the bringing. God knew what He was doing when He brought you two together.

Reflection Question: How does knowing God brought you together change your perspective?

DAY 174

"Let your fountain be blessed: and rejoice with the wife of thy youth." – Proverbs 5:18 (KJV)

Your fountain—your source of refreshment, life, and joy—needs blessing, not neglect. How do you bless your fountain? Through gratitude, investment, and protection.

Rejoicing isn't past tense. Keep rejoicing with the spouse of your youth, even as youth fades. Find new reasons to rejoice. Create fresh occasions for celebration. Let rejoicing be your default setting. Bless your fountain. Rejoice in your choice. Keep celebrating what you have.

Reflection Question: How can you bless your fountain today?

DAY 175

"Her children arise up, and call her blessed; her husband also, and he praiseth her." – Proverbs 31:28 (KJV)

Public praise matters. When others hear you praising your spouse—especially your children—it creates family culture. You're teaching what love looks like, what respect sounds like, what honor acts like.

Don't wait for special occasions to praise. Make it regular, specific, and genuine. "Your mom is amazing because..." "Your dad blessed us by..." Let praise be the soundtrack of your home.

Rise up and call your spouse blessed. Let everyone hear it.

Reflection Question: Who needs to hear you praise your spouse today?

DAY 176

"But from the beginning of the creation God made them male and female." – Mark 10:6 (KJV)

Your differences are by design, not defect. God made you different on purpose—to complement, not compete. Where you're weak, they're often strong. Where they struggle, you might excel.

Stop trying to make your spouse more like you. Their different perspective isn't wrong, just different. Their different approach isn't inferior, just distinct. Celebrate the design instead of fighting it. You weren't meant to be identical but interconnected.

Reflection Question: What difference in your spouse can you celebrate as design?

DAY 177

"If two lie together, then they have heat: but how can one be warm alone?"
– Ecclesiastes 4:11 (KJV)

Warmth in marriage isn't just physical but emotional and spiritual. You warm each other through presence, not just proximity. Through connection, not just coexistence.

Some seasons are cold—financially, emotionally, spiritually. That's when you need each other's warmth most. Don't withdraw when winter comes; draw closer. Your combined heat can survive any cold.

Lie together—figuratively and literally. Share warmth. You're each other's heating system.

Reflection Question: Where does your marriage need more warmth?

DAY 178

"Let all bitterness, and wrath, and anger, and clamour, and evil speaking, be put away from you, with all malice: And be ye kind one to another." –
Ephesians 4:31-32 (KJV)

Bitterness is marriage poison—slow-acting but lethal. It starts small, grows quietly, then destroys suddenly. That resentment you're nursing? It's not hurting them; it's killing you.

Put it away means active removal, not passive hoping it disappears. Dig out the root of bitterness before it produces fruit. Replace it with kindness—the antidote to anger, the cure for clamour. Clean house emotionally. Evict bitterness and install kindness.

Reflection Question: What bitterness needs putting away from your marriage?

DAY 179

*"I will sing of mercy and judgment: unto thee, O LORD, will I sing." –
Psalm 101:1 (KJV)*

Your marriage needs both mercy and judgment—mercy for failures, judgment for wisdom. Sing of both. Celebrate when mercy covers mistakes. Appreciate when good judgment prevents problems.

Don't be all mercy (enabling) or all judgment (condemning). Find the rhythm between grace and truth, forgiveness and accountability, acceptance and growth. Sing a balanced song in your marriage. Let mercy and judgment harmonize.

Reflection Question: Which does your marriage need more of right now—mercy or judgment?

DAY 180

*"My dove, my undefiled is but one; she is the only one of her mother." –
Song of Solomon 6:9 (KJV)*

Your spouse is one of a kind—literally irreplaceable. There's no backup, no substitute, no plan B. They're your "only one," unique and undefiled by comparison.

Stop measuring them against others. They're not competing; they've already won by being chosen. Celebrate their uniqueness instead of trying to standardize them.

You got the only one like them. Treat them accordingly.

Reflection Question: What makes your spouse uniquely "the only one" for you?

DAY 181

"Lo, children are an heritage of the LORD: and the fruit of the womb is his reward." – Psalm 127:3 (KJV)

If you have children, they're not interruptions to your marriage but investments in it. They're heritage—legacy builders, love multipliers, and union proof. Your love created life.

If you don't have children, your marriage still bears fruit—spiritual children, mentored couples, impacted lives. Your union produces heritage in different forms.

Whether biological or spiritual, your marriage is producing heritage. Celebrate the fruit.

Reflection Question: What heritage is your marriage producing?

July: Deepening Roots

Day 182

"But let patience have her perfect work, that ye may be perfect and entire, wanting nothing." – James 1:4 (KJV)

July's heat tests everything—gardens wilt, tempers flare, and patience evaporates faster than morning dew. Your marriage might feel that pressure too. Here's the secret: patience isn't just waiting; it's what you do while waiting.

Think about slow-cooked barbecue—the kind that takes all day. You could microwave that meat in minutes, but it wouldn't have the same depth, tenderness, or flavor. Your spouse is slow-cooking into who God designed them to be. Some transformations can't be rushed.

That habit you wish they'd change? That dream they're chasing? That healing they need? Patience says, "I'll wait with you, not just for you." It's active presence, not passive endurance.

Perfect work takes time. Your marriage is becoming "entire, wanting nothing"—but not overnight.

Reflection Question: What area of growth in your spouse requires your patient presence?

DAY 183

"He that is slow to anger is better than the mighty; and he that ruleth his spirit than he that taketh a city." – Proverbs 16:32 (KJV)

You know that moment when your spouse says the wrong thing at the worst time? Your blood boils, words load like ammunition, and war feels inevitable. But ruling your spirit in that moment is more powerful than any argument you could win. It's like holding fire and choosing not to throw it. Anyone can explode; true strength is redirecting that energy. The real warrior isn't the one who wins arguments but the one who prevents wars. Your spouse needs a partner who rules their spirit, not one ruled by it. Master yourself before trying to manage your marriage.

Reflection Question: When is it hardest for you to rule your spirit with your spouse?

DAY 184

"The words of a wise man's mouth are gracious; but the lips of a fool will swallow up himself." – Ecclesiastes 10:12 (KJV)

Ever said something to your spouse and instantly wished you could take it back? Like trying to put toothpaste back in the tube—impossible and messy. Foolish words don't just hurt you; they disrupt your marriage's peace. Gracious words, however, are like good seasoning—they enhance everything. "Thanks for making dinner" tastes better than silence. "I appreciate you" goes down easier than criticism. Your mouth can serve a feast of grace or a platter of problems. Today, before you speak, season your words. Make them so gracious you'd gladly eat them yourself.

Reflection Question: What gracious words has your spouse been hungry to hear?

DAY 185

"Take us the foxes, the little foxes, that spoil the vines: for our vines have tender grapes." – Song of Solomon 2:15 (KJV)

It's not usually the big things that wreck marriages—it's the little foxes. The way they leave cabinets open. The tone they use when stressed. The phone scrolling during conversations. Small annoyances that nibble away at love's vineyard.

These little foxes sneak in unnoticed. One day you're madly in love; next thing you know, you're just mad. Those tender grapes of affection got spoiled while you weren't watching.

Time to go fox hunting. Identify those small irritants before they become big resentments. Catch them, address them, or choose to ignore them—but don't let them spoil your vine.

Reflection Question: What "little fox" is spoiling your marriage vineyard?

DAY 186

"Be not hasty in thy spirit to be angry: for anger resteth in the bosom of fools." – Ecclesiastes 7:9 (KJV)

Anger in marriage is like leaving milk on the counter in July—it spoils everything quickly. That hasty anger you felt this morning? It's probably resting in your chest right now, curdling into something worse. Notice it says anger "rests" in fools—it moves in, unpacks, and makes itself comfortable. In wise people, anger visits but doesn't stay. It knocks, delivers its message, then leaves. Don't give anger a guest room in your marriage.

Feel it, acknowledge it, then evict it. Your bosom has better things to host—like love, peace, and joy.

Reflection Question: What anger has overstayed its welcome in your marriage?

DAY 187

"He that troubleth his own house shall inherit the wind." – Proverbs 11:29 (KJV)

Some people are married to their spouse but trouble their own house—creating drama, picking fights, stirring pots that should simmer peacefully. It's like drilling holes in your own boat then wondering why you're sinking. Troubling your house looks like bringing work stress home, punishing your spouse for other people's actions, or creating problems because you're bored. You inherit wind—lots of noise and destruction, but nothing you can hold. Be a peace-maker in your own home. Build instead of troubling. You'll inherit substance instead of wind.

Reflection Question: How might you be troubling your own house?

DAY 188

"For ye have need of patience, that, after ye have done the will of God, ye might receive the promise." – Hebrews 10:36 (KJV)

You've been praying for your marriage, working on yourself, trying to improve things. Where's the breakthrough? Why isn't change happening faster? Welcome to the waiting room between obedience and promise. It's like planting tomatoes— you prep soil, plant seeds, water faithfully, then... nothing. For weeks. But underground, invisible to impatient eyes, roots are spreading, stems are strengthening. The promise is coming; it just isn't microwave-ready. Keep doing God's will in your marriage even when you don't see results. The promise is as sure as God's word.

Reflection Question: What promise are you waiting to see fulfilled in your marriage?

DAY 189

"The discretion of a man deferreth his anger; and it is his glory to pass over a transgression." – Proverbs 19:11 (KJV)

Your spouse just did that thing—you know, THAT thing they always do. Your anger is locked and loaded. But what if your glory is found in passing over it? Like a parade marshal who sees the mistake but keeps the parade moving.

Discretion chooses which battles deserve energy. Not every transgression needs a response. Some things are better passed over than picked apart. It's not weakness; it's wisdom. You're choosing peace over proving points. Today, try passing over something you'd normally pounce on. See if glory follows.

Reflection Question: What transgression could you gloriously pass over today?

DAY 190

"My son, hear the instruction of thy father, and forsake not the law of thy mother." – Proverbs 1:8 (KJV)

Your parents taught you about marriage—intentionally or accidentally, positively or negatively. Some lessons need keeping; others need tossing. The key is knowing which is which.

Maybe Dad showed you patience, but also workaholism. Perhaps Mom demonstrated loyalty, but also enabling. Take the gold, leave the dross. Your marriage doesn't need to repeat their mistakes or reject their wisdom wholesale.

Learn from the past without living in it. Your parents' marriage was their story; you're writing yours.

Reflection Question: What parental lesson about marriage needs keeping or releasing?

DAY 191

"Open rebuke is better than secret love." – Proverbs 27:5 (KJV)

That difficult conversation you're avoiding? Your spouse needs to hear it. Secret love—the kind that won't speak truth to prevent pain—isn't as loving as it seems. It's like knowing they have spinach in their teeth but saying nothing to avoid awkwardness.

Open rebuke wrapped in love beats silent resentment every time. "Honey, this bothers me" is better than suffering silently until you explode. Your spouse can't fix what they don't know is broken. Love them enough to speak truth, even when it's uncomfortable.

Reflection Question: What loving truth does your spouse need to hear?

DAY 192

"The soul of the sluggard desireth, and hath nothing: but the soul of the diligent shall be made fat." – Proverbs 13:4 (KJV)

Lazy marriages desire intimacy but won't work for it. They want connection without conversation, passion without pursuit, depth without digging. Like wanting a garden while refusing to pull weeds.

Diligent marriages do the work—the daily choosing, the consistent kindness, the intentional intimacy. They get "fat" with satisfaction because they invested effort. Your marriage won't accidentally become amazing; it requires diligence. Stop wishing and start working. Diligent souls get what sluggards only dream about.

Reflection Question: Where has laziness crept into your marriage efforts?

DAY 193

"And if one prevail against him, two shall withstand him; and a threefold cord is not quickly broken." – Ecclesiastes 4:12 (KJV)

Life's coming at you fast—bills, kids, stress, health issues. Alone, you might crumble. But two? You can withstand. Add God as your third cord? Now you're unbreakable.

Picture a rope made of three strands. Pull on one strand alone, it snaps. Weave three together, and you could tow a truck. Your marriage is designed for that kind of strength—not independent threads but interwoven cords. Whatever's prevailing against you right now, face it together. You're stronger than you think.

Reflection Question: What challenge requires your threefold cord strength right now?

DAY 194

"She girdeth her loins with strength, and strengtheneth her arms." – Proverbs 31:17 (KJV)

Strength in marriage isn't just emotional—it's choosing to be strong for your relationship. Like going to the gym, not because you love burpees but because you love being healthy. Both spouses need this kind of intentional strengthening.

Girding your loins meant preparing for work or battle. Some days, marriage requires both. Strengthen your arms—your ability to hold, help, and heal. Get strong enough to carry your load and occasionally theirs too.

Don't wait for strength to find you. Gird up, strengthen up, show up strong.

Reflection Question: What area of strength does your marriage need you to develop?

DAY 195

"Even a fool, when he holdeth his peace, is counted wise." – Proverbs 17:28 (KJV)

Sometimes the wisest thing you can say to your spouse is nothing. That comeback locked and loaded? Swallow it. That "I told you so" dancing on your tongue? Let it die there.

Silence can be more powerful than speeches. It gives anger time to cool, wisdom space to arrive, and your spouse room to think. You might not be the wisest person, but holding your peace makes you look like it. Try strategic silence today. Let your spouse have the last word. See what happens when you choose quiet over quick responses.

Reflection Question: When should you hold your peace instead of speaking your piece?

DAY 196

"Thou wilt keep him in perfect peace, whose mind is stayed on thee: because he trusteth in thee." – Isaiah 26:3 (KJV)

Your marriage stress might be stealing your sleep. Finances, future, fears—they're all swirling in your mind like a tornado. But perfect peace isn't found in perfect circumstances; it's found in staying your mind on God.

It's like adjusting your TV antenna (remember those?). All that static clears when you find the right position. Stay your mind on God's faithfulness, not your spouse's failures. Focus on His promises, not your problems.

Perfect peace is available, even in imperfect marriages. Trust and stay focused.

Reflection Question: What worry needs to be replaced with trust in God?

DAY 197

"Let another praise thee, and not thine own mouth; a stranger, and not thine own lips." – Proverbs 27:2 (KJV)

Nobody likes the spouse who constantly says, "I'm such a good husband" or "I'm an amazing wife." But when others hear YOUR spouse praising you? That carries weight. Be the public relations department for your spouse's reputation.

Tell others about their victories. Brag about their growth. Let strangers know how blessed you are. Your spouse needs to know they're winning in your eyes, and others need to hear it from your lips. Stop advertising your own marriage achievements. Start announcing theirs.

Reflection Question: Who needs to hear you praise your spouse today?

DAY 198

"A time to rend, and a time to sew; a time to keep silence, and a time to speak." – Ecclesiastes 3:7 (KJV)

Timing in marriage is everything. The right words at the wrong time are still wrong. It's like trying to sew while the fabric is still tearing—you need to stop the damage first.

Sometimes your marriage needs rending—tearing down old patterns. Sometimes it needs sewing—stitching wounds closed. Wisdom knows which season you're in. Don't try to fix what God's still revealing. Don't stay silent when it's time to speak up.

Read the room. Know your season. Time your words wisely.

Reflection Question: Is this a time for silence or speaking in your marriage situation?

DAY 199

"Where there is no vision, the people perish." – Proverbs 29:18 (KJV)

What's your five-year marriage plan? Ten-year? If you don't know where you're going together, you'll end up nowhere in particular. Marriage without vision is just two people aging in the same house.

Vision isn't about perfect planning but purposeful direction. Where do you want to be spiritually, emotionally, financially? What legacy are you building? What dreams are you chasing together? Without vision, your marriage is slowly perishing from purposelessness. Dream together. Plan together. Create vision before you need it.

Reflection Question: What vision do you need to create for your marriage?

DAY 200

"He that hath pity upon the poor lendeth unto the LORD." – Proverbs 19:17 (KJV)

When your spouse is poor—in spirit, energy, patience, or hope—your pity (compassion) is a loan to God. He pays back with interest. That grace you extend when they're emotionally bankrupt? God's keeping track.

Sometimes your spouse is rich and can give. Sometimes they're poor and need to receive. Don't keep score of who's been poor longest. Just have pity, show mercy, extend credit. God's good for the repayment.

See your spouse's poverty as opportunity for divine investment.

Reflection Question: Where is your spouse "poor" and needing your compassion?

DAY 201

"He that is slow to wrath is of great understanding." – Proverbs 14:29 (KJV)

Quick anger reveals shallow understanding. When your spouse triggers instant wrath, you're probably not understanding their heart, their hurt, or their history. Slow down. There's always more to the story.

Like developing film (ancient reference!), understanding takes time to develop. That thing your spouse just did probably connects to something deeper. Their reaction might be about fear, not defiance. Their words might mask hurt, not harbor hatred.

Great understanding comes to those who postpone wrath long enough to ask, "What's really happening here?"

Reflection Question: What triggers your quick wrath that needs slower understanding?

DAY 202

"Train up a child in the way he should go: and when he is old, he will not depart from it." – Proverbs 22:6 (KJV)

Your marriage is training your children (or others watching) about relationships. They're learning conflict resolution from your arguments, affection from your interactions, commitment from your choices. You're writing their marriage manual through your example. What are you teaching? That love quits when things get hard? Or that love perseveres? That marriage is misery? Or that it's worth fighting for? Your marriage is someone's training ground. Live like future marriages depend on your example—because they do.

Reflection Question: What marriage lesson are others learning from watching you?

DAY 203

"But if any provide not for his own, and specially for those of his own house, he hath denied the faith." – 1 Timothy 5:8 (KJV)

Provision isn't just financial—it's emotional, spiritual, and physical. Are you providing safety, encouragement, and affection? Your spouse needs more than money; they need your presence, attention, and investment.

Some spouses are financially rich but emotionally bankrupt. They provide houses but not homes, things but not time, stuff but not security. Don't deny the faith by neglecting provision's fuller meaning. Provide what money can't buy—your full presence and genuine care.

Reflection Question: What non-financial provision does your spouse need from you?

DAY 204

"To him that knoweth to do good, and doeth it not, to him it is sin." – James 4:17 (KJV)

You know what would bless your spouse. That chore they hate. That word they need. That gesture that speaks love. Knowing without doing is sin—not just missed opportunity but willful neglect.

It's like walking past a glass of water when you know they're thirsty. The sin isn't in what you do wrong but in good you leave undone. Your marriage has enough challenges without adding sins of omission. Do the good you know to do. Today. Before knowing becomes sinning.

Reflection Question: What good are you knowing but not doing for your spouse?

DAY 205

"The fear of man bringeth a snare." – Proverbs 29:25 (KJV)

Are you more concerned about what others think of your marriage than what God thinks? That social media pressure to look perfect? That family opinion you're trying to manage? It's a snare, trapping you in performance instead of authenticity.

Your marriage doesn't need to impress anyone except the One who created it. Stop performing for people who aren't living your life. Their approval won't warm your bed or weather your storms.

Fear God's opinion alone. Everyone else is just noise.

Reflection Question: Whose opinion about your marriage has become a snare?

DAY 206

"And let us not be weary in well doing: for in due season we shall reap, if we faint not." – Galatians 6:9 (KJV)

Marriage kindness can feel like farming in drought—lots of sowing, no showing. You keep serving, forgiving, trying, but where's the harvest? Don't quit now. Due season is coming, and it's always later than we want but sooner than we expect.

That spouse who seems unchanged by your efforts? Seeds are germinating underground. That situation that won't budge? Roots are spreading where you can't see. Keep doing good even when good seems pointless.

Don't faint at mile 25 of this marathon. The finish line is closer than you think.

Reflection Question: Where do you need encouragement to keep doing good?

DAY 207

"The wrath of a king is as messengers of death: but a wise man will pacify it." – Proverbs 16:14 (KJV)

When your spouse is royally angry (we all have those king or queen moments), you have choices. Match their wrath? Run? Or be wise and pacify? Pacifying isn't cowering—it's strategic peace-making.

Like a skilled negotiator defusing a bomb, wisdom knows which wire to cut. Sometimes it's humor. Sometimes it's space. Sometimes it's a gentle answer. But wisdom always chooses de-escalation over detonation.

Be the wise one who pacifies wrath before it delivers death to your peace.

Reflection Question: How can you wisely pacify your spouse's wrath when it rises?

DAY 208

"Heaviness in the heart of man maketh it stoop: but a good word maketh it glad." – Proverbs 12:25 (KJV)

Your spouse might be stooping under invisible weight—worry, disappointment, exhaustion. You can see it in their shoulders, their shuffle, their sigh. They need a good word like medicine.

"You're doing great." "I'm proud of you." "We'll get through this together." Simple words, powerful impact. Like helium to a deflating balloon, good words lift heavy hearts. You have the power to make gladness from heaviness.

Speak that good word. Watch them rise.

Reflection Question: What good word could lift your spouse's heavy heart?

DAY 209

"He that covereth his sins shall not prosper: but whoso confesseth and forsaketh them shall have mercy." – Proverbs 28:13 (KJV)

That thing you're hiding from your spouse—it's not protected, it's festering. Like an infected wound under a bandage, covered sins don't heal; they spread. Your marriage can't prosper with secrets between you.

Confession is terrifying but liberating. "I need to tell you something" might be the hardest and best sentence you speak. Mercy waits on the other side of confession, but you have to walk through honesty to get there.

Uncover what you've been hiding. Confess, forsake, find mercy.

Reflection Question: What needs confessing in your marriage?

DAY 210

"The righteous is more excellent than his neighbour." – Proverbs 12:26 (KJV)

Your righteousness (right living) affects your spouse more than anyone else. When you choose integrity, they benefit. When you pursue godliness, they're blessed. Your excellence elevates their experience.

This isn't about being better than your spouse but being better FOR your spouse. Your spiritual growth is a gift to your marriage. Every step toward righteousness is a step toward relational excellence.

Be more excellent. Not for competition but for contribution.

Reflection Question: How does your righteousness benefit your spouse?

DAY 211

"He that is faithful in that which is least is faithful also in much." – Luke 16:10 (KJV)

Those small marriage promises matter more than you think. Calling when you said you would. Taking out trash without reminders. Small faithfulness builds big trust.

Your spouse is watching your faithfulness in tiny things, determining if you're trustworthy with their whole heart. It's like a trust thermometer—every kept promise raises the temperature.

Be faithful in the least. Text when you're running late. Keep small promises. Build big trust.

Reflection Question: What "least" thing needs your faithfulness today?

DAY 212

"A good name is rather to be chosen than great riches." – Proverbs 22:1 (KJV)

Your marriage has a reputation. What do people think when they hear your names together? Drama? Stability? Love? Conflict? You're building a name with every interaction, every public moment, every visible choice.

That reputation affects everything—your children's security, your ministry impact, your legacy. Guard your marriage's name like the treasure it is. Don't sell it for temporary satisfaction or momentary victory.

Choose a good name over being right, over getting even, over proving points.

Reflection Question: What reputation is your marriage building?

AUGUST: HARVESTING JOY

DAY 213

"He that goeth forth and weepeth, bearing precious seed, shall doubtless come again with rejoicing, bringing his sheaves with him." – Psalm 126:6 (KJV)

August is harvest time, but remember—every harvest started with someone crying while planting. Those tears you've shed over your marriage? They weren't wasted. They watered seeds you couldn't see growing.

Maybe you planted forgiveness through tears of hurt. Perhaps you sowed patience while weeping over disappointment. Like a farmer who plants in sorrow but reaps in joy, your emotional investment is about to pay dividends.

Those sheaves (bundles of blessing) are coming. You can doubt many things, but don't doubt this: tearful planting leads to joyful harvesting.

Reflection Question: What tears from your past are becoming today's harvest?

DAY 214

"Be of good courage, and he shall strengthen your heart, all ye that hope in the LORD." – Psalm 31:24 (KJV)

Courage in marriage isn't the absence of fear—it's choosing connection despite it. It takes courage to stay vulnerable after being hurt, to trust after betrayal, to hope after disappointment. Here's the promise: when you show courage, God provides strength. It's like stepping onto a bridge you can't see the end of—each courageous step reveals more solid ground. Your heart gets stronger not by avoiding risk but by taking godly chances. Be courageous today. Have that conversation. Take that step. God's got your heart.

Reflection Question: Where does your marriage need your courage?

DAY 215

"A man's belly shall be satisfied with the fruit of his mouth; and with the increase of his lips shall he be filled." – Proverbs 18:20 (KJV)

You're eating your words in marriage—literally living in the atmosphere your mouth creates. Speak criticism? You'll digest discord. Speak encouragement? You'll feast on favor. Your lips are producing increase or decrease, satisfaction or starvation. That complaint you voiced this morning? You'll taste it at dinner. That compliment you gave? It's seasoning everything sweetly. Want a more satisfying marriage? Change the menu of your words.

Reflection Question: What words are you feeding your marriage?

DAY 216

"Go thy way, eat thy bread with joy, and drink thy wine with a merry heart; for God now accepteth thy works." – Ecclesiastes 9:7 (KJV)

Stop waiting for perfect circumstances to enjoy your marriage. God accepts your works—your effort, your progress, your imperfect but sincere attempts. Time to celebrate what you have, not mourn what you lack.

Eat your ordinary bread with joy. Turn Tuesday dinner into a celebration. Drink your regular morning coffee with a merry heart. Find reasons to feast in the everyday, because God's already pleased with your efforts. Joy doesn't require perfection, just permission. Give yourself permission to enjoy your marriage now.

Reflection Question: What ordinary moment can you celebrate with joy today?

DAY 217

"Therefore shall a man leave his father and his mother, and shall cleave unto his wife: and they shall be one flesh." – Genesis 2:24 (KJV)

Leaving and cleaving is a lifelong process, not a wedding day event. You might still be emotionally attached to your family's approval, financially dependent on their help, or constantly comparing your marriage to theirs.

True cleaving requires complete leaving. Like transplanting a tree—it can't thrive in new soil while roots remain in old ground. Your marriage needs space to grow its own root system. Check your roots. Are they fully transplanted, or are you still drawing from old soil?

Reflection Question: What root still needs transplanting from your family of origin?

DAY 218

"I will both lay me down in peace, and sleep: for thou, LORD, only makest me dwell in safety." – Psalm 4:8 (KJV)

Bedtime in marriage can be battlefield or sanctuary. Are you taking today's tensions to bed, or laying them down in peace? That evening rehashing of problems—is it helping or just stealing sleep?

God offers safety for your marriage bed—not just physical but emotional. You can both lay down in peace when you trust Him with your problems. Stop trying to solve everything before sleep. Some solutions come better with rest. Make your bed a peace zone. Arguments can wait until morning.

Reflection Question: What needs to be laid down for peaceful sleep tonight?

DAY 219

"There is that scattereth, and yet increaseth; and there is that withholdeth more than is meet, but it tendeth to poverty." – Proverbs 11:24 (KJV)

Generosity in marriage multiplies mysteriously. The more affection you scatter, the more you have. The more grace you give, the richer you become. But withhold what your spouse needs, and you both grow poor.

It's like trying to hoard sunshine—the tighter you grip, the less you hold. But open your hands, scatter freely, and somehow you end up with more. Give compliments generously. Scatter kindness wildly. Watch increase follow.

Stop withholding what costs you nothing but blesses everything.

Reflection Question: What are you withholding that needs scattering?

DAY 220

"There is no fear in love; but perfect love casteth out fear." – 1 John 4:18 (KJV)

What fear is contaminating your marriage? Fear of vulnerability? Fear of repeating past mistakes? Fear of not being enough? These fears create walls where God intended bridges.

Perfect love—not perfect performance but perfect acceptance—evicts fear like light dismisses darkness. When your spouse knows they're perfectly loved (flaws included), their fears start packing. When you rest in their perfect love, your anxieties relocate. Love perfectly (completely, not flawlessly). Watch fear flee.

Reflection Question: What fear needs evicting through perfect love?

DAY 221

"The heart of her husband doth safely trust in her, and he shall have no need of spoil." – Proverbs 31:11 (KJV)

Trust is marriage's oxygen—invisible but essential. Can your spouse's heart safely rest with you? Are their secrets secure, their vulnerabilities protected, their weaknesses covered?

Safe trust means they don't need backup plans (spoil). They're not emotionally shopping elsewhere, seeking validation from others, or keeping escape routes open. Your trustworthiness makes them rich in security. Be a safe deposit box for your spouse's heart. Guard what they entrust to you.

Reflection Question: How can you make your spouse's heart safer with you?

DAY 222

"The way of a fool is right in his own eyes: but he that hearkeneth unto counsel is wise." – Proverbs 12:15 (KJV)

Your spouse's perspective might be the counsel you need but don't want. When they suggest a different approach, do you defend or listen? Their outside view of your inside situation could be wisdom disguised as criticism.

It's like trying to cut your own hair—you need someone else's eyes to see the back. Your spouse sees angles of you that you can't. Their counsel might sting, but it could also save. Stop being right in your own eyes. Hearken to your built-in counselor.

Reflection Question: What counsel from your spouse have you been resisting?

DAY 223

"He that walketh with wise men shall be wise: but a companion of fools shall be destroyed." – Proverbs 13:20 (KJV)

Who's influencing your marriage? Those friends who encourage divorce at every difficulty? That relative who criticizes your spouse constantly? You become like your companions, and your marriage reflects their influence.

Seek wise marriage mentors. Spend time with couples who've weathered storms. Let their wisdom rub off through proximity. Distance yourself from fools who plant discord and harvest destruction. Your marriage needs wise companions more than comfortable ones.

Reflection Question: Which relationships strengthen or weaken your marriage?

DAY 224

"Pleasant words are as an honeycomb, sweet to the soul, and health to the bones." – Proverbs 16:24 (KJV)

Your words can be medicine or poison to your marriage. Pleasant words don't mean fake sweetness—they mean choosing honey over vinegar, even when addressing sour situations.

"We need to talk" hits different than "I'd love to figure this out together." Same message, different medicine. Your spouse's soul needs sweetness, their bones need health that pleasant words provide.

Become a honey factory, not a vinegar vineyard. Sweet words heal what harsh ones hurt.

Reflection Question: What pleasant words could bring health to your spouse today?

DAY 225

"Pride goeth before destruction, and an haughty spirit before a fall." – Proverbs 16:18 (KJV)

That need to be right in every argument? Pride. That refusal to apologize first? Haughty spirit. They're setting your marriage up for a fall, like climbing a ladder with broken rungs.

Humility might feel like losing, but it's actually winning at what matters. Would you rather be right or be married? Pride chooses right; wisdom chooses relationship.

Check your pride levels. Is it worth the coming destruction?

Reflection Question: Where is pride setting up your marriage for a fall?

DAY 226

"Can a man take fire in his bosom, and his clothes not be burned?" –
Proverbs 6:27 (KJV)

That "harmless" flirtation at work? That emotional connection with someone online? That comparison of your spouse to others? You're playing with fire, thinking you won't get burned.

Fire in your bosom always burns—if not you, then your marriage. Those clothes (your covenant covering) will catch flame. No one handles fire without consequences, no matter how controlled they think they are.

Drop the matches. Walk away from sparks. Your marriage can't survive the burns.

Reflection Question: What fire needs to be extinguished before it burns?

DAY 227

"Her ways are ways of pleasantness, and all her paths are peace." – *Proverbs 3:17 (KJV)*

Wisdom makes marriage pleasant, not perfect. Her paths lead to peace, not paradise. Following God's wisdom for relationships creates an atmosphere where love thrives.

Are your ways pleasant? Do your paths lead to peace or problems? That sharp tongue might win arguments but loses atmosphere. That stubborn streak might prove points but destroys peace.

Choose wisdom's ways. Make pleasantness your method, peace your destination.

Reflection Question: Which of your ways needs wisdom's pleasant makeover?

DAY 228

"Every wise woman buildeth her house: but the foolish plucketh it down with her hands." – Proverbs 14:1 (KJV)

Building and plucking can happen simultaneously. You might be building financially while plucking down emotionally. Building reputation while destroying intimacy. Both spouses can build or pluck—wisdom chooses construction.

Every criticism plucks a brick. Every encouragement places one. Every cold shoulder removes support beams. Every warm embrace reinforces foundations. Check your hands—are they building or demolishing?

Build more than you pluck. Your house depends on it.

Reflection Question: What have your hands been plucking that needs building?

DAY 229

"Better is a dry morsel, and quietness therewith, than an house full of sacrifices with strife." – Proverbs 17:1 (KJV)

That lavish lifestyle you're killing yourselves to maintain—is it worth the marital strife? Sometimes less is more when less comes with peace. A simple meal in harmony beats a feast in fighting.

Downsizing isn't defeat if it ups your peace. That smaller house might mean bigger happiness. That simpler lifestyle might create richer relationships. Stop sacrificing peace for prosperity. Choose quietness over quantity. Your marriage needs peace more than pieces.

Reflection Question: What could you simplify to increase marital peace?

DAY 230

"Let all things be done decently and in order." – 1 Corinthians 14:40 (KJV)

Chaos in marriage creates stress. When nothing has order—finances scattered, responsibilities unclear, communication chaotic—everything feels harder. Decency and order aren't boring; they're breathing room.

Like a messy kitchen makes cooking harder, marital disorder makes loving harder. Who handles what? When do you connect? How do you decide? Order answers these, creating space for spontaneity within structure.

Bring order to one chaotic area. Watch stress decrease, peace increase.

Reflection Question: What area of marriage chaos needs decent order?

DAY 231

"Let your moderation be known unto all men." – Philippians 4:5 (KJV)

Marriage extremes exhaust everyone. All work, no play. All intensity, no rest. All serious, no silly. Moderation creates sustainability—a pace you can maintain for decades, not just days.

Your spouse needs moderate you—not perfect or terrible, just steady. Consistent kindness beats sporadic grand gestures. Regular presence beats occasional perfection.

Find your middle ground. Extreme marriages tend to extremely end.

Reflection Question: Where does your marriage need more moderation?

DAY 232

"And be not conformed to this world: but be ye transformed by the renewing of your mind." – Romans 12:2 (KJV)

The world's marriage manual reads differently than God's. Culture says "follow your heart"; God says "guard it." Society preaches "you deserve happiness"; Scripture teaches "serve one another."

Stop conforming to relationship rules that aren't working for anyone. That 50% divorce rate? That's worldly wisdom. Transform your marriage mind through God's word, not world's ways.

Different is good when different is godly.

Reflection Question: What worldly marriage pattern needs transforming?

DAY 233

"For God is not the author of confusion, but of peace." – 1 Corinthians 14:33 (KJV)

If your marriage feels confusing, God didn't write that chapter. Mixed signals, unclear expectations, emotional chaos—these aren't from Him. He authors peace, even in life's difficult paragraphs.

Confusion often comes from too many authors. Whose advice are you following? Whose voice is loudest? When God's not the primary author, the story gets convoluted.

Let God write your marriage story. His plotlines always lead to peace.

Reflection Question: What confusion needs God's peaceful authorship?

DAY 234

"Honour thy father and thy mother: that thy days may be long." – Exodus 20:12 (KJV)

Honoring parents while cleaving to spouse requires balance. You can respect where you came from while building where you're going. Honor doesn't mean obedience to parents over spouse.

Show your children how to honor parents by how you treat yours—and your spouse's. But also show them that marriage creates a new primary loyalty. Honor the past, prioritize the present.

Balance honor with healthy boundaries.

Reflection Question: How can you honor parents while prioritizing your spouse?

DAY 235

"A brother offended is harder to be won than a strong city." – Proverbs 18:19 (KJV)

Once you've deeply offended your spouse, winning them back is like conquering a fortified city. Their walls go up, gates lock, and trust becomes a lengthy siege. Better to avoid offense than attempt conquest.

Watch your words and actions. That joke at their expense? That public embarrassment? That betrayed confidence? These build walls that take years to demolish.

Prevent fortification through careful consideration.

Reflection Question: What might be building walls in your spouse's heart?

DAY 236

"By much slothfulness the building decayeth; and through idleness of the hands the house droppeth through." – Ecclesiastes 10:18 (KJV)

Marriage maintenance isn't optional. Like a house needs regular repairs, relationships need consistent care. Ignore the little leaks, and eventually the roof caves in.

Slothfulness in marriage looks like coasting on past efforts, assuming love maintains itself, neglecting small gestures. These create slow decay that suddenly becomes collapse.

Do maintenance before you need major repairs.

Reflection Question: What marriage maintenance have you been neglecting?

DAY 237

"Trust in the LORD with all thine heart; and lean not unto thine own understanding." – Proverbs 3:5 (KJV)

Your understanding of marriage is limited by your experience. Maybe you've only seen dysfunction. Perhaps you're copying patterns that don't work. Your understanding isn't enough for marriage's complexity.

Trust God's design over your assumptions. His ways might seem counterintuitive—serve to lead, die to live, give to receive. But His understanding sees the full picture while yours sees fragments.

Lean on eternal wisdom, not temporary understanding.

Reflection Question: Where are you leaning on limited understanding?

DAY 238

"Let thy waters be dispersed abroad, and rivers of waters in the streets." –
Proverbs 5:16 (KJV)

Your marriage should overflow with such love that others get splashed. Not broadcasting intimate details, but radiating joy that refreshes everyone around you.

When marriages are healthy, they water their communities. Your love becomes others' hope. Your unity inspires their effort. Your joy reminds them it's possible.

Let your love overflow. Dry marriages surround you, needing your rivers.

Reflection Question: How can your marriage water others around you?

DAY 239

"And above all these things put on charity, which is the bond of perfectness."
– Colossians 3:14 (KJV)

Charity (love) is marriage's super glue—bonding what seems unbondable, perfecting what appears unfixable. It's the overlay that makes everything else work together.

You might have communication, attraction, and compatibility, but without charity binding them, they're just loose pieces. Love is the bond that creates perfection from imperfect parts.

Put on charity like a coat that covers everything else.

Reflection Question: Where does your marriage need charity's bonding power?

DAY 240

"Let us therefore follow after the things which make for peace." – Romans 14:19 (KJV)

Peace doesn't happen accidentally—you follow after it, pursue it, chase it down. Every choice either leads toward peace or away from it. That tone, that topic, that timing—is it making for peace?

Following peace might mean dropping the subject, changing your approach, or waiting for better timing. It's actively choosing paths that lead to harmony over being heard.

Make peace your marriage's GPS destination.

Reflection Question: What path would lead to more peace today?

DAY 241

"Faithful are the wounds of a friend; but the kisses of an enemy are deceitful." – Proverbs 27:6 (KJV)

Your spouse's honest feedback might wound, but it's faithful. They see your blind spots, know your weaknesses, and love you enough to speak truth. Those wounds heal stronger.

Beware of those who only tell you what you want to hear about your marriage. Their kisses (flattery) might feel better than your spouse's wounds (truth), but they're deceitful.

Welcome faithful wounds over false kisses.

Reflection Question: What faithful wound from your spouse needs accepting?

DAY 242

"He that answereth a matter before he heareth it, it is folly and shame unto him." – Proverbs 18:13 (KJV)

Stop formulating your response while your spouse is still talking. That rebuttal you're crafting? It's folly. You're answering a matter you haven't fully heard, preparing defense against partial information.

Really hearing means listening to understand, not to respond. It's catching their heart, not just their words. When you answer before hearing, you're basically saying, "I don't need to hear you to know I'm right."

Listen fully, then answer thoughtfully.

Reflection Question: When do you most often answer before truly hearing?

DAY 243

"Blessed are the peacemakers: for they shall be called the children of God." – Matthew 5:9 (KJV)

Making peace in marriage is divine work. Not peacekeeping (avoiding conflict) but peacemaking (resolving it). It's actively building bridges where walls exist.

Peacemakers don't take sides; they take hands. They don't assign blame; they assume responsibility. They don't win arguments; they win unity. This is God's children's work—bringing heaven's peace to earth's relationships.

Be a peacemaker in your own marriage. Start with your own conflicts.

Reflection Question: Where can you shift from peacekeeping to peacemaking?

September: Seasons of Change

Day 244

"To every thing there is a season, and a time to every purpose under the heaven." – Ecclesiastes 3:1 (KJV)

September whispers change—leaves beginning their color shift, kids returning to school, summer's heat giving way to autumn's coolness. Your marriage has seasons too, and fighting them is like wearing shorts in a snowstorm.

Maybe you're grieving the season of young kids ending, or anxiously awaiting an empty nest. Perhaps you miss when date nights were spontaneous, not scheduled between soccer practices. Here's the thing: every season serves a purpose. Winter marriages need deeper roots. Spring marriages need room to bloom. Summer marriages need pruning. Fall marriages need to let some things go.

Stop mourning the season that's ending and start asking what this new one offers. That career change? That health challenge? It's not interrupting your marriage—it's introducing a new season.

Reflection Question: What new season is your marriage entering, and what might be its purpose?

DAY 245

"Two are better than one; because they have a good reward for their labour." – Ecclesiastes 4:9 (KJV)

Ever tried assembling furniture alone? Wrestling an Allen wrench, juggling pieces, and wondering why you didn't wait for help? Marriage turns solo wrestling into teamwork. Your spouse sees the step you missed, holds the piece you can't reach, and laughs when you're ready to toss the manual. Life's "assembly required"—raising kids, building careers, creating homes—gets easier with four hands instead of two. But here's the key: being "better together" means actually working together, not just sharing space. When you share the labor, the reward doubles.

Reflection Question: What task have you been attempting alone that needs four hands?

DAY 246

"A soft answer turneth away wrath: but grievous words stir up anger." – Proverbs 15:1 (KJV)

Your spouse walks in with storm clouds in their eyes—work was awful, traffic worse, and they're searching for lightning rods. You have two choices: be the rod or the diffuser. "Rough day?" lands softer than "What's your problem?" "Tell me about it" beats "Not this again." It's verbal aikido—redirecting negative energy instead of meeting force with force. Like adding water to a boiling pot instead of cranking the heat. Soft doesn't mean weak; it means choosing de-escalation over destruction, conversation over confrontation. Your soft answer might be the only gentle thing they experience all day.

Reflection Question: What soft answer could replace your typical harsh response?

DAY 247

"Be not wise in thine own eyes: fear the LORD, and depart from evil." –
Proverbs 3:7 (KJV)

Know what's exhausting? Being the self-appointed marriage expert who sees all the problems, has all the answers, and knows exactly what your spouse should change. That "wisdom" might actually be near-sightedness in disguise. Like using a 1995 map, you know some things but miss crucial updates. God's wisdom includes roads you haven't discovered, shortcuts you haven't considered, and destinations you can't imagine. Maybe your spouse's different approach isn't wrong—just different. Maybe God is using their weakness to reveal your pride.

Reflection Question: Where have you been too wise in your own eyes?

DAY 248

"Better is a handful with quietness, than both hands full with travail and
vexation of spirit." – Ecclesiastes 4:6 (KJV)

That couple with the perfect house, perfect kids, perfect Instagram feed? Look closer. Full hands often hide empty hearts. You're comparing your handful to their apparent armfuls, forgetting that your quietness might be worth more than their chaos. Some couples have everything but peace—designer kitchens where no one cooks together, luxury vacations filled with arguments, success that costs more than it gives. Your "handful"—a modest home, simple joys, real conversations—might be the true treasure. Stop chasing "both hands full" if it means losing quietness. Some upgrades aren't upgrades at all.

Reflection Question: What "handful with quietness" are you undervaluing?

DAY 249

"Where no oxen are, the crib is clean: but much increase is by the strength of the ox." – Proverbs 14:4 (KJV)

Want a perfectly clean, conflict-free marriage? Stay single. The moment you add another person, you add mess—emotional mess, physical mess, complicated mess. But you also add strength, increase, and possibility.

Your spouse's annoying habits are like ox droppings—evidence of life and labor. That wet towel on the bed, that different spending philosophy, that way they load the dishwasher "wrong"—it's proof you have an ox, a partner, someone sharing the load. Clean cribs are overrated. Embrace the beautiful mess of two lives becoming one.

Reflection Question: What "mess" is actually evidence of life and partnership?

DAY 250

"He that is slow to anger is better than the mighty; and he that ruleth his spirit than he that taketh a city." – Proverbs 16:32 (KJV)

That moment when your spouse pushes your button—the one connected directly to your temper? Ruling your spirit then is harder than conquering nations. But it's also more valuable.

Think about it: anyone can explode. Toddlers do it professionally. But controlling that explosion, channeling that energy into understanding instead of attack? That's mighty. It's like catching a baseball barehanded—it stings, but you prevented greater damage. Your spouse needs a partner who rules their spirit, not one ruled by every emotion.

Reflection Question: When is it hardest to rule your spirit with your spouse?

DAY 251

"Let nothing be done through strife or vainglory; but in lowliness of mind let each esteem other better than themselves." – Philippians 2:3 (KJV)

Who gets credit for the good in your marriage? Who takes blame for the bad? If you're keeping score, you're playing the wrong game. Marriage isn't about individual stats but team wins. Esteeming your spouse better doesn't mean you're worse—it means choosing to spotlight their strengths over your own. Like a photographer who makes everyone else look good while staying behind the camera. Your spouse shines brighter when you're holding the light. Try this: for one day, give them all the credit. See what happens.

Reflection Question: How can you esteem your spouse better than yourself today?

DAY 252

"Whoso keepeth his mouth and his tongue keepeth his soul from troubles." – Proverbs 21:23 (KJV)

That thing you're about to say—the zinger, the complaint, the "constructive criticism"—swallow it. Your mouth is writing checks your marriage can't afford to cash. Some words cost more than they're worth. It's like sending an email when you're angry—satisfying for three seconds, regrettable for three weeks. Your tongue has the power to create troubles that take months to untangle. But kept in check, it keeps your soul (and marriage) from unnecessary drama. Practice the pause. Count to ten. Better to keep your mouth than lose your peace.

Reflection Question: What words need keeping rather than speaking?

DAY 253

"A merry heart doeth good like a medicine: but a broken spirit drieth the bones." – Proverbs 17:22 (KJV)

When did laughter leave your marriage? Not polite chuckles but real, deep, can't-breathe laughter? Life got serious, responsibilities mounted, and somewhere joy got buried under duty. Resurrect the ridiculous. Dance badly in the kitchen. Share that embarrassing story again. Watch comedy instead of drama. Your marriage needs medicine, and laughter is free, available, and has zero side effects except happiness. A broken spirit dries everything—conversation, intimacy, hope. But a merry heart? It heals what you didn't know was sick.

Reflection Question: How can you prescription laughter for your marriage today?

DAY 254

"Let no corrupt communication proceed out of your mouth, but that which is good to the use of edifying." – Ephesians 4:29 (KJV)

Your words are either construction workers or demolition crews. Every conversation builds or bulldozes. "You always" and "you never" are wrecking balls. "I appreciate" and "thank you" lay foundations.

Corrupt communication isn't just cursing—it's corroding comments that rust your relationship. Sarcasm that stings. Jokes that aren't funny. Tone that cuts. These create invisible damage that becomes visible over time. Build with your words. Your marriage needs construction, not destruction.

Reflection Question: What corrupt communication needs replacing with edification?

DAY 255

"Iron sharpeneth iron; so a man sharpeneth the countenance of his friend."
– Proverbs 27:17 (KJV)

Sharpening creates friction—sparks fly, metal heats, pressure applies. Your spouse sharpening you doesn't feel comfortable, but comfort doesn't create cutting-edge character.

They see your dull spots—where you've grown lazy, compromised, or settled. Their friction isn't attack; it's refinement. Like a knife that's lost its edge, you need someone close enough to sharpen you, invested enough to apply pressure. Embrace the sparks. They're not burning your marriage; they're making it sharper.

Reflection Question: What sharpening from your spouse are you resisting?

DAY 256

"For where your treasure is, there will your heart be also." – Matthew 6:21
(KJV)

Check your calendar and credit card statement—they're GPS coordinates for your heart. If work gets prime time and your spouse gets leftovers, your treasure map needs adjusting.

Investing in your marriage doesn't mean expensive getaways (though those are nice). It means treasuring Tuesday night conversations over Thursday night overtime. It means putting your phone down when they're talking. It means choosing presence over presents. Your heart follows your investment. Invest in your spouse, watch your heart follow.

Reflection Question: Where is your treasure, and is your spouse finding your heart there?

DAY 257

"He that covereth a transgression seeketh love; but he that repeateth a matter separateth very friends." – Proverbs 17:9 (KJV)

That thing your spouse did three years ago—why does it keep appearing in arguments? Like reheating old food, repeatedly serving past failures makes everyone sick.

Covering transgressions doesn't mean ignoring issues—it means once addressed, they're buried, not exhumed for ammunition. Love covers, protects, and moves forward. Repeating matters is like picking scabs—it prevents healing and leaves scars.

Stop rehearsing their failures. Start covering with love.

Reflection Question: What past matter needs permanent covering?

DAY 258

"The discretion of a man deferreth his anger; and it is his glory to pass over a transgression." – Proverbs 19:11 (KJV)

Not every offense needs a response. Sometimes glory comes from letting things go—like a parade continuing despite someone dropping their baton. The show goes on, dignity intact.

Your spouse will transgress—leave socks on the floor, forget important dates, say thoughtless things. Discretion chooses which hills are worth dying on. Most aren't. Glory comes from gracefully passing over what would previously provoke.

Be glorious today. Pass over something you'd normally pounce on.

Reflection Question: What transgression can you gloriously pass over?

DAY 259

"She looketh well to the ways of her household, and eateth not the bread of idleness." – Proverbs 31:27 (KJV)

Looking well to your household means seeing what needs attention before it becomes emergency. Both spouses can do this—noticing emotional climates, relationship temperature, and family dynamics.

Idleness in marriage isn't just physical laziness—it's emotional coasting, spiritual complacency, relational autopilot. While you're eating the bread of idleness, problems are growing like weeds in an untended garden.

Stay alert. Your household needs someone looking well to its ways.

Reflection Question: What way of your household needs better looking after?

DAY 260

"A word fitly spoken is like apples of gold in pictures of silver." – Proverbs 25:11 (KJV)

Timing transforms words from noise to treasure. "I love you" during an argument hits different than during affection. "I'm sorry" immediately means more than "I'm sorry" next week.

Fitly spoken means right word, right time, right tone. Like a photographer waiting for perfect lighting, wisdom waits for the right moment. Your words could be golden apples, but served at the wrong time, they're just fruit falling on deaf ears.

Practice timing. Make your words treasures, not just sounds.

Reflection Question: What word needs better timing to become treasure?

DAY 261

"Who can find a virtuous woman? for her price is far above rubies." –
Proverbs 31:10 (KJV)

Stop searching for what you already found. Your spouse might not match Proverbs 31 perfectly (who does?), but they're your ruby—precious, unique, and increasing in value.

The question "who can find" implies rarity. You found rare. Now the question becomes: are you treating rare like common? Are you polishing your ruby or letting it gather dust? Virtue in marriage grows with recognition and appreciation.

You've got rubies. Stop shopping for rhinestones.

Reflection Question: What virtue in your spouse have you been overlooking?

DAY 262

"Hatred stirreth up strifes: but love covereth all sins." – Proverbs 10:12 (KJV)

Love is the ultimate concealer—covering blemishes, mistakes, and imperfections. Not hiding them, but choosing not to expose them. Like a photographer using soft lighting instead of harsh fluorescents.

Every marriage has sins needing covering—thoughtless words, selfish choices, human failures. Hatred exposes and magnifies; love covers and minimizes. Your choice determines your marriage atmosphere: courtroom or sanctuary.

Choose love's covering over hatred's exposing.

Reflection Question: What sin in your marriage needs love's covering?

DAY 263

"A foolish son is the calamity of his father: and the contentions of a wife are a continual dropping." – Proverbs 19:13 (KJV)

Continual dropping drives people crazy—drip, drip, drip of constant complaints, corrections, and contentions. Both spouses can create this water torture. That repeated reminder, that constant criticism, that never-ending narrative of what's wrong.

Here's the thing: even legitimate complaints become background noise when constant. Your spouse stops hearing and starts enduring. Like living near train tracks—eventually, you don't notice the noise, just feel the vibration.

Stop the drip. Say it once, clearly, then stop.

Reflection Question: Where have you become a continual dropping?

DAY 264

"It is better to dwell in the wilderness, than with a contentious and an angry woman." – Proverbs 21:19 (KJV)

Making home a place your spouse wants to escape isn't the goal. Yet sometimes our contention creates wilderness from what should be oasis. Both spouses can make home feel like exile.

Ask yourself: is my presence peaceful or punishing? Do they look forward to coming home or finding reasons to stay away? Wilderness might be lonely, but at least it's quiet. Don't make solitude more attractive than your company. Create oasis, not wilderness, with your presence.

Reflection Question: Does your presence make home feel like wilderness or oasis?

DAY 265

"The aged women likewise, that they be in behaviour as becometh holiness...
That they may teach the young women to be sober, to love their husbands."
– Titus 2:3-4 (KJV)

Loving your spouse is both instinct and instruction, natural and learned. Who's teaching you? What examples are you following? Not everyone married long has been married well.

Find couples who've weathered decades and still like each other. Learn their secrets, their systems, their survival strategies. But also become teachers yourselves—someone's watching your marriage for hope. Love is learned. Keep learning, start teaching.

Reflection Question: Who can teach you to love your spouse better?

DAY 266

"Likewise, ye wives, be in subjection to your own husbands; that, if any obey not the word, they also may without the word be won by the conversation of the wives." – 1 Peter 3:1 (KJV)

Actions preach louder than arguments. Your life testimony might reach your spouse where your words can't. This applies to both spouses—sometimes silent witness wins where verbal witnessing fails.

"Conversation" here means conduct, lifestyle, behavior. Your spouse watches how you handle stress, treat others, respond to problems. They're reading your life like a book, and sometimes that story converts better than sermons. Live the change you want to see.

Reflection Question: What is your conduct preaching to your spouse?

DAY 267

"Set a watch, O LORD, before my mouth; keep the door of my lips." –
Psalm 141:3 (KJV)

Your mouth needs security—someone checking what goes out before damage occurs. Like airport security for your words, screening for dangerous items that could hijack your peace.

Ask God to be your security guard. Before speaking, let Him scan your words for weapons—sarcasm, criticism, complaints. Let Him confiscate what could harm your marriage. Some words shouldn't board the plane of conversation.

Install divine security at your lips.

Reflection Question: What words need confiscating before they escape?

DAY 268

"Be kindly affectioned one to another with brotherly love; in honour preferring one another." – Romans 12:10 (KJV)

Preferring your spouse means choosing their restaurant when you're craving something else. It's watching their show when yours is on. It's celebrating their promotion when yours was overlooked.

This isn't doormat behavior—it's love behavior. When both prefer the other, everyone wins. Like two people trying to give each other the bigger piece of cake—sweetness multiplies in the giving.

Prefer your spouse today in something specific.

Reflection Question: Where can you prefer your spouse's preference?

DAY 269

"Wherefore, my beloved brethren, let every man be swift to hear, slow to speak, slow to wrath." – James 1:19 (KJV)

Most marriage conflicts happen because we reverse this order—slow to hear, swift to speak, quick to wrath. Like trying to drive in reverse on the highway—dangerous and ineffective.

Swift hearing means catching not just words but hearts. Slow speaking means thinking before reacting. Slow wrath means counting to ten, then twenty, then maybe sleeping on it. This formula prevents more fights than any counseling session. Practice the order: hear first, speak second, wrath last (if at all).

Reflection Question: Which part of this formula do you most often reverse?

DAY 270

"Nevertheless let every one of you in particular so love his wife even as himself; and the wife see that she reverence her husband." – Ephesians 5:33 (KJV)

Men need respect like oxygen; women need love like water. Not stereotypes but general truths. When she feels cherished, she flourishes. When he feels respected, he rises. Both need both, but primary needs differ.

Love looks like security, gentleness, and priority. Respect looks like admiration, trust, and honor. Stop giving what you need; start giving what they need. It's like speaking their native language instead of expecting them to always translate. Learn your spouse's primary language.

Reflection Question: Does your spouse need more love or more respect today?

DAY 271

"And they were both naked, the man and his wife, and were not ashamed."
– Genesis 2:25 (KJV)

True intimacy requires nakedness—not just physical but emotional. No hiding behind performance, pretense, or perfection. Just two people, fully exposed, fully accepted.

Shame builds walls where God intended oneness. Past wounds create cover-ups. Fear fashions masks. But real connection requires vulnerability—showing scars, sharing struggles, revealing reality.

Eden's innocence might be lost, but its intimacy is still available.

Reflection Question: Where does shame prevent nakedness in your marriage?

DAY 272

"My beloved is mine, and I am his." – Song of Solomon 2:16 (KJV)

Mutual belonging—you're not losing yourself but finding yourself in belonging. Your spouse is yours, you are theirs. Not possession but partnership, not ownership but stewardship.

This belonging brings both privilege and responsibility. Privilege to be chosen, cherished, claimed. Responsibility to protect, provide, and pursue. You belong to each other in ways you belong to no one else.

Celebrate your mutual belonging.

Reflection Question: How can you celebrate belonging to each other?

DAY 273

"Her husband is known in the gates, when he sitteth among the elders of the land." – Proverbs 31:23 (KJV)

Your spouse's reputation is partially in your hands. How you speak about them publicly either builds or destroys their standing. That "harmless" complaint to friends, that eye roll when they're talking—people notice.

Make your spouse "known in the gates" for good reasons. Be their publicity agent, not their critic. Share their victories more than their failures. Make others wish they had what you have, not wonder why you stay.

Build their reputation with your words.

Reflection Question: How are you affecting your spouse's public reputation?

October: Deeper Still

Day 274

"And the LORD God said, It is not good that the man should be alone; I will make him an help meet for him." – Genesis 2:18 (KJV)

Before sin entered, before problems existed, God declared aloneness "not good." You were designed for partnership—not just roommates splitting rent but soul-deep companionship that makes life richer.

October strips trees bare, revealing structure underneath. Sometimes marriage needs that same unveiling—seeing past the leaves of routine to the trunk of truth: you need each other. Not just for tasks but for completeness. Your spouse isn't your accessory; they're your answer to cosmic loneliness.

"Help meet" means suitable helper—perfectly matched to your specific needs. Like a custom-made puzzle piece, your spouse fits where others couldn't.

Reflection Question: How is your spouse the perfect "help meet" for your specific needs?

DAY 275

"Let her own husband render unto the wife due benevolence: and likewise also the wife unto the husband." – 1 Corinthians 7:3 (KJV)

"Due benevolence" sounds like paying taxes, but it's really about generous giving. Your spouse is due your kindness, affection, and attention—not as payment but as privilege.

Think of it like this: you water plants not because they demand it but because that's how gardens grow. Your marriage needs regular benevolence—kind words, gentle touches, focused attention. Not grand gestures but consistent kindness.

What's due isn't minimum payment but maximum blessing.

Reflection Question: What benevolence is due to your spouse today?

DAY 276

"Drink waters out of thine own cistern, and running waters out of thine own well." – Proverbs 5:15 (KJV)

Stop looking over the fence at other wells. That water might look cleaner, taste sweeter, or flow easier, but it's not yours. Your own cistern contains everything you need—you just might need to dig deeper.

Your spouse is a deep well of possibility. You've maybe drawn from the surface, but there are depths unexplored. New conversations await. Hidden talents exist. Unexpressed dreams lie buried. Stop thirsting after foreign wells when yours runs deep.

Drink deeply from what you have.

Reflection Question: What depths in your spouse remain unexplored?

DAY 277

"Therefore shall a man leave his father and his mother, and shall cleave unto his wife." – Genesis 2:24 (KJV)

Leaving is a journey, not just a moving day. You might have left physically but still be emotionally tethered, mentally comparing, or financially dependent. True leaving creates space for true cleaving.

Like a boat that can't sail while tied to the dock—you can start the engine, make noise, create waves, but you're not going anywhere. Cut the ropes. Not to dishonor where you came from but to honor where you're going.

Your marriage needs you fully present, not partially anchored elsewhere.

Reflection Question: What ties to your past are preventing full cleaving?

DAY 278

"Live joyfully with the wife whom thou lovest all the days of the life of thy vanity, which he hath given thee under the sun." – Ecclesiastes 9:9 (KJV)

Life is vapor—here then gone. Your days together are numbered, not to create panic but purpose. Why waste them in misery? Joy is available if you'll choose it.

Living joyfully doesn't require perfect circumstances—just purposeful choices. Laugh at the chaos. Dance in the kitchen. Make memories from mundane moments. Your life might be vanity (temporary), but your joy can be substantial.

Choose joy while you have days to choose.

Reflection Question: How can you live more joyfully with your spouse today?

DAY 279

"Many waters cannot quench love, neither can the floods drown it." – Song of Solomon 8:7 (KJV)

Your love has survived storms—financial floods, health hurricanes, family tornadoes. If it was quenchable, it would've died already. But here you are, still choosing each other.

Love that survives floods comes out purified. Like gold refined by fire, your relationship is stronger for surviving struggles. Those "many waters" that threatened to drown you? They've actually deepened your anchor.

Your love is flood-proof. Trust its durability.

Reflection Question: What flood has your love already survived?

DAY 280

"Husbands, love your wives, even as Christ also loved the church, and gave himself for it." – Ephesians 5:25 (KJV)

Christ's love wasn't theoretical—it was thorns, nails, and sacrifice. This is the model for marriage: love that gives when it's hard, serves when it's inconvenient, sacrifices when it costs.

This applies to both spouses. Love that gives itself doesn't calculate returns. It doesn't keep spreadsheets of who gave more. It pours out knowing that giving is its own reward. Your spouse needs this kind of love—not perfect but sacrificial.

Give yourself to your marriage like Christ gave Himself.

Reflection Question: What sacrifice does your love need to make?

DAY 281

"Whoso findeth a wife findeth a good thing, and obtaineth favour of the Lord." – Proverbs 18:22 (KJV)

You didn't just find a spouse—you obtained divine favor. Like winning a lottery you didn't know you entered. God's favor came wrapped in human form, probably in pajamas right now.

Stop treating favor like burden. Your spouse is God's good gift, even when they're grumpy, even when they're difficult, even when they're human. The favor isn't in their perfection but in their presence.

You found good. Start treating it that way.

Reflection Question: How is your spouse God's favor in your life?

DAY 282

"Let the husband render unto the wife due benevolence: and likewise also the wife unto the husband." – 1 Corinthians 7:3 (KJV)

Due benevolence is ongoing debt—you never fully pay it off. Every day, you owe kindness, patience, and affection. Not burden but blessing, not obligation but opportunity.

Like a subscription service to love—automatic renewal, regular delivery, consistent service. Your spouse subscribed to you for life. Keep delivering what they signed up for: benevolence, blessing, and belonging.

Pay what's due with interest.

Reflection Question: What benevolence payment is overdue?

DAY 283

"Let thy fountain be blessed: and rejoice with the wife of thy youth." –
Proverbs 5:18 (KJV)

That young couple who got married—they're still in there
somewhere. Under the stress, beyond the stretch marks,
beneath the responsibilities. The ones who stayed up talking
until dawn, who couldn't keep their hands off each other.

Rejoice with that person. Not in spite of who they've become
but because of it. Your fountain needs blessing, not criticism.
Water it with appreciation, protect it with faithfulness, celebrate it with joy.

Youth might fade, but rejoicing shouldn't.

*Reflection Question: What about "the spouse of your youth" still
makes you rejoice?*

DAY 284

*"And if a house be divided against itself, that house cannot stand." – Mark
3:25 (KJV)*

Division in marriage rarely happens suddenly—it's small cracks
that spread. Different dreams pulling opposite directions. Separate lives under one roof. Two individuals forgetting they're
one team.

Check your foundation. Are you united in purpose? Supporting
each other publicly? Fighting for your marriage or with each
other? Division starts subtly—separate bank accounts become
separate hearts.

Unite before you divide.

*Reflection Question: Where is division creeping into your
house?*

DAY 285

"Submitting yourselves one to another in the fear of God." – Ephesians 5:21 (KJV)

Mutual submission—both yielding, both serving, both considering the other. Not one person always bending but both choosing flexibility. Like dance partners taking turns leading.

Submit to their expertise in their areas. Submit to their needs when yours can wait. Submit to their dreams when yours have had spotlight. This isn't weakness but wisdom—recognizing you're both valuable, both have insight, both deserve honor.

Practice mutual submission today.

Reflection Question: Where can you submit to your spouse's wisdom?

DAY 286

"Her children arise up, and call her blessed; her husband also, and he praiseth her." – Proverbs 31:28 (KJV)

Public praise hits different than private compliments. When others hear you celebrating your spouse—especially your children—it creates family culture. You're teaching what love looks like.

Don't wait for Mother's Day or birthdays. Rise up randomly and call them blessed. Let everyone hear how blessed you feel. Make praise the soundtrack of your home, not criticism the background noise.

Arise and bless, publicly and often.

Reflection Question: Who needs to hear you praise your spouse?

DAY 287

"A virtuous woman is a crown to her husband: but she that maketh ashamed is as rottenness in his bones." – Proverbs 12:4 (KJV)

You're either a crown or corruption to your spouse—adding honor or creating shame. This applies to both partners. Your behavior becomes their reputation. Your character affects their confidence.

Being a crown means making them proud to claim you. Not perfection but progression. Not flawlessness but faithfulness. When people meet you, do they understand why your spouse chose you?

Be the crown your spouse deserves to wear.

Reflection Question: Are you being a crown or creating shame?

DAY 288

"It is not good that the man should be alone." – Genesis 2:18 (KJV)

Loneliness in marriage hurts worse than single solitude—you're together but alone. Sharing space but not souls. Present but not connected.

God didn't just solve physical aloneness with marriage—He addressed existential isolation. Your spouse needs more than your presence; they need your participation. More than coexistence; they need connection.

Bridge the gap. Your spouse might be alone with you right there.

Reflection Question: Where might your spouse feel alone despite your presence?

DAY 289

"I am my beloved's, and my beloved is mine." – Song of Solomon 6:3 (KJV)

Possession without possessiveness—you belong to each other without owning each other. It's security without suffocation, belonging without bondage.

"I am my beloved's"—completely given. "My beloved is mine"—completely received. This mutual belonging creates safety. You're off the market, unavailable, spoken for. That security should create freedom, not fear.

Belong boldly. You're taken and given simultaneously.

Reflection Question: How can you demonstrate belonging without being possessive?

DAY 290

"She will do him good and not evil all the days of her life." – Proverbs 31:12 (KJV)

Consistency matters more than intensity. Doing good "all the days"—Monday through Sunday, January through December, honeymoon through hardship. Not perfect days but persistent choice.

Good looks like patience on bad days. Evil looks like weaponizing weaknesses. Good builds; evil breaks. This applies to both spouses—choosing their good over your mood, their benefit over your bitterness.

Do good especially when you don't feel good.

Reflection Question: How can you do good when feeling bad?

DAY 291

"Let love be without dissimulation." – Romans 12:9 (KJV)

Fake love exhausts everyone. Pretending everything's fine when it's not. Performing for others while dying inside. Dissimulation is exhausting disguise.

Real love admits struggle while maintaining commitment. It says, "This is hard, but you're worth it." It drops masks, risks reality, chooses authenticity over appearance. Your spouse needs real you, not role-play you.

Love genuinely, not generically.

Reflection Question: Where has your love become performance?

DAY 292

"She openeth her mouth with wisdom; and in her tongue is the law of kindness." – Proverbs 31:26 (KJV)

Wisdom knows what to say; kindness knows how to say it. Both spouses need this combination—truth without brutality, honesty without harshness.

The law of kindness means kindness rules every word. Even correction comes wrapped in compassion. Even confrontation includes care. Your tongue can enforce kindness or break its law.

Make kindness your mouth's constitution.

Reflection Question: Does wisdom or kindness need more practice in your speech?

DAY 293

"So ought men to love their wives as their own bodies. He that loveth his wife loveth himself." – Ephesians 5:28 (KJV)

You wouldn't punch yourself in the face, so why wound your spouse with words? You're one flesh—hurting them is self-harm. Their pain becomes yours, eventually.

Love your spouse with the same instinctive care you give yourself. Feed them when hungry. Comfort when hurting. Protect from harm. It's not sacrifice—it's self-preservation. You're caring for your own body.

Love them like you love yourself—automatically, consistently, protectively.

Reflection Question: How is loving your spouse actually self-care?

DAY 294

"The heart of her husband doth safely trust in her." – Proverbs 31:11 (KJV)

Safe trust means your spouse's secrets are secure. Their vulnerabilities won't become weapons. Their confessions won't become ammunition. Their hearts can rest without guard.

Can your spouse trust you with their fears? Their dreams? Their struggles? Or do they edit, filter, and protect themselves from you? Safe trust creates space for real intimacy.

Be the vault where your spouse's heart finds safety.

Reflection Question: Is your spouse's heart safe with you?

DAY 295

"Let all bitterness, and wrath, and anger, and clamour, and evil speaking, be put away from you." – Ephesians 4:31 (KJV)

Bitterness is marriage poison—slow-acting but lethal. It starts as hurt, ferments into resentment, and eventually becomes hatred. That thing you can't let go? It's poisoning everything.

Put it away means active removal. Like taking out trash—it stinks, but leaving it inside makes everything smell. Bitterness belongs in the dump, not your heart. Your marriage can't breathe with that toxic air.

Take out the trash. All of it.

Reflection Question: What bitterness needs immediate removal?

DAY 296

"For this cause shall a man leave father and mother, and shall cleave to his wife." – Mark 10:7 (KJV)

Every holiday, every decision, every conflict tests your leaving and cleaving. Whose traditions win? Whose opinions matter most? Where does loyalty lie?

Cleaving means choosing your spouse when families clash. Not dishonoring parents but prioritizing partner. Your new family needs its own culture, not just inherited patterns. You're writing a new story, not copying old chapters.

Leave fully to cleave completely.

Reflection Question: Where do you need to choose cleaving over old patterns?

DAY 297

"My beloved is white and ruddy, the chiefest among ten thousand." – Song of Solomon 5:10 (KJV)

In your eyes, your spouse should be "chiefest among ten thousand"—not perfect but preferred. Not flawless but favorite. The world offers ten thousand options, but you've chosen one.

Stop comparing your one to the ten thousand. They don't need to be best objectively, just best for you. Celebrate what makes them chief in your eyes—their laugh, their loyalty, their love.

Make them feel chosen, not settled for.

Reflection Question: What makes your spouse "chiefest" in your eyes?

DAY 298

"Be ye therefore merciful, as your Father also is merciful." – Luke 6:36 (KJV)

Your spouse needs mercy like they need oxygen—constantly, consistently, abundantly. Mercy for mistakes, mercy for moods, mercy for humanity. God's mercy toward you is the model.

Mercy sees the failure but chooses compassion. It could demand justice but offers grace. Your marriage needs more mercy than justice, more grace than grievance.

Be merciful especially when they don't deserve it—that's when it's most like God's.

Reflection Question: Where does your spouse need your mercy most?

DAY 299

"A friend loveth at all times, and a brother is born for adversity." –
Proverbs 17:17 (KJV)

Your spouse should be your best friend, not just your lover. Friends laugh together, share secrets, enjoy hanging out. When did you last just enjoy their company without agenda?

But they're also born for adversity—designed by God to stand with you through storms. They're not fair-weather friends but all-weather allies. In prosperity and poverty, sickness and health—sound familiar?

Be the friend who loves at all times.

Reflection Question: How can you be a better friend to your spouse?

DAY 300

"But I say unto you, Love your enemies, bless them that curse you." –
Matthew 5:44 (KJV)

Sometimes your spouse feels like the enemy. In those moments—when you're hurt, angry, feeling attacked—God says love anyway. Bless when you want to blast.

This isn't about being a doormat but about being like Jesus. He loved those who crucified Him. You can love your spouse even when they're being difficult. It's supernatural love, not natural reaction.

Love when they're unloveable. That's when love matters most.

Reflection Question: How can you love when your spouse feels like an enemy?

DAY 301

"He that troubleth his own house shall inherit the wind." – Proverbs 11:29 (KJV)

Creating drama in your own home is like setting fire to your own bed—you'll sleep in the ashes. Some people trouble their house with criticism, complaints, and chaos, then wonder why peace left.

Stop troubling your own house. That need to be right, to stir things up, to create excitement through conflict—it's destroying what you're trying to build. You'll inherit wind—lots of noise, no substance.

Be a peacemaker in your own home.

Reflection Question: How might you be troubling your own house?

DAY 302

"Who can find a virtuous woman? for her price is far above rubies... Her husband is known in the gates." – Proverbs 31:10,23 (KJV)

Your virtue affects your spouse's reputation. When you live with integrity, they're honored by association. When you compromise, they're contaminated by connection.

This applies to both spouses. Your character becomes their calling card. How you behave at work affects how they're viewed at church. Your social media presence impacts their social standing.

Live virtuously for your spouse's sake, not just your own.

Reflection Question: How does your virtue affect your spouse's reputation?

DAY 303

"And they twain shall be one flesh." – Mark 10:8 (KJV)

One flesh is progressive—you're more unified now than on your wedding day. Every shared experience weaves you tighter. Every overcome obstacle binds you closer. You're becoming what you committed to being.

But oneness requires intention. You can live parallel lives in the same house or intertwined lives in unity. Choose to weave together rather than unravel apart.

Celebrate your increasing oneness.

Reflection Question: How have you become more "one flesh" this year?

DAY 304

"Marriage is honourable in all, and the bed undefiled." – Hebrews 13:4 (KJV)

October ends with reminder: your marriage is honorable. Not perfect but honorable. Not easy but worthy. God honors what culture dismisses.

Keep your marriage bed undefiled—physically, emotionally, spiritually. No third parties, no comparisons, no pollution. What happens between you is sacred, whether society agrees or not.

Honor what God honors. Your marriage matters more than you know.

Reflection Question: How can you better honor what God has joined?

NOVEMBER: GRATITUDE AND GRACE

DAY 305

"In every thing give thanks: for this is the will of God in Christ Jesus concerning you." – 1 Thessalonians 5:18 (KJV)

November naturally turns thoughts toward gratitude, but "in everything" includes that annoying habit your spouse has. Yes, even the way they squeeze toothpaste from the middle. Even how they're always five minutes late. Everything.

Here's the plot twist: thanking God for your spouse's quirks changes how you see them. That perpetual lateness? Maybe it's because they're always doing one more thing for someone else. That toothpaste chaos? At least they're brushing. Gratitude doesn't ignore annoyances—it reframes them.

God's will isn't that everything be perfect, but that you find thankfulness anyway. Your spouse gives you daily opportunities to practice this supernatural gratitude. Lucky you.

Reflection Question: What irritating trait in your spouse might actually be a blessing in disguise?

DAY 306

"Let your speech be alway with grace, seasoned with salt." – Colossians 4:6 (KJV)

Think of your words like Thanksgiving dinner—grace is the main course, salt is the seasoning. Too much salt ruins everything. No salt makes it bland. You need both, properly balanced. "Honey, we need to talk about the budget" lands better than "You're spending us into bankruptcy!" Same truth, different seasoning. Grace makes hard truths digestible. Salt preserves the message from being forgotten. Your spouse needs both—truth they can swallow and remember. Season your words today like you're preparing a feast, not fast food.

Reflection Question: Are your words over-salted or under-seasoned with grace?

DAY 307

"As we have therefore opportunity, let us do good unto all men, especially unto them who are of the household of faith." – Galatians 6:10 (KJV)

Your spouse is your first "household of faith"—your primary ministry, your closest neighbor. Yet sometimes we're kinder to strangers than to the person sharing our bed. We give our best at work and our leftovers at home. That opportunity to do good? It's brewing coffee before they wake up. It's taking their car for gas so they don't have to. It's doing good especially to them, not eventually if you have time. They're not just "all men"—they're your person. Do good at home first.

Reflection Question: What good have you been doing for others that your spouse needs?

DAY 308

"Forbearing one another, and forgiving one another, if any man have a quarrel against any: even as Christ forgave you, so also do ye." – Colossians 3:13 (KJV)

Forbearing is pre-forgiveness—putting up with stuff before it even becomes an offense. It's like wearing emotional shock absorbers in marriage. Your spouse is going to bump into you; forbearance keeps it from becoming a collision. That quarrel you have? Compare it to what Christ forgave you for. Suddenly their failure to take out trash seems less criminal. They forgot your anniversary? You forgot God for years. Perspective changes everything. Christ's forgiveness of you is the measuring stick for forgiving them. Forbear more, quarrel less.

Reflection Question: What do you need to forbear rather than fight about?

DAY 309

"Give her of the fruit of her hands; and let her own works praise her in the gates." – Proverbs 31:31 (KJV)

Your spouse's efforts deserve recognition—public, specific, and sincere. Not generic "thanks for everything" but "Thank you for how you handled that difficult conversation with our teenager yesterday." Let their works praise them through your words. Both spouses need this. See what they do, say what you see, celebrate their contribution. That presentation they nailed at work? Praise it. That meal they cooked? Acknowledge it. That patience they showed? Highlight it. Give them credit for the fruit they're producing.

Reflection Question: What specific work of your spouse needs public praise?

DAY 310

"Better is a dinner of herbs where love is, than a stalled ox and hatred therewith." – Proverbs 15:17 (KJV)

You could have steak every night, but if you're eating in angry silence, you're starving. Meanwhile, someone's sharing ramen noodles with genuine laughter and deep conversation—they're feasting.

Stop waiting for perfect circumstances to be happy. That dream house won't fix your marriage. That promotion won't create connection. Love transforms whatever's on the table into a banquet. Hatred makes even luxury taste like cardboard. Choose love over luxury. It's the secret sauce that makes everything better.

Reflection Question: What simple meal could become a feast with added love?

DAY 311

"She riseth also while it is yet night, and giveth meat to her household." – Proverbs 31:15 (KJV)

Rising while it's still night isn't about becoming a morning person—it's about anticipating needs before they're expressed. Both spouses can do this: seeing what's needed and providing before being asked.

Your spouse shouldn't have to beg for attention, affection, or appreciation. Rise early (figuratively) to meet their needs. Be proactive in love. That thing they always have to ask for? Do it before they ask. That need they have? Meet it before they mention it. Love anticipates; it doesn't wait for requests.

Reflection Question: What need can you meet before your spouse has to ask?

DAY 312

"If we confess our sins, he is faithful and just to forgive us our sins, and to cleanse us from all unrighteousness." – 1 John 1:9 (KJV)

That thing you're hiding from your spouse—it's growing in the dark like mold. Confession brings it into light where healing happens. "I need to tell you something" might be terrifying, but it's also liberating.

God's faithfulness in forgiving you shows your spouse how to forgive you. If the Creator can cleanse your unrighteousness, your spouse can work through your mistake. But confession has to come first. No confession, no cleansing. No honesty, no healing. Whatever you're hiding is hurting your intimacy.

Reflection Question: What needs confessing for cleansing to begin?

DAY 313

"But the wisdom that is from above is first pure, then peaceable, gentle, and easy to be intreated." – James 3:17 (KJV)

Heavenly wisdom for marriage isn't complicated—be pure in motive, peaceable in approach, gentle in delivery, and easy to be entreated (approachable, flexible). It's wisdom that bends without breaking.

When your spouse comes with a concern, are you easy to be entreated or impossible to approach? Do you dig in your heels or remain flexible? Wisdom from above prioritizes peace over position, gentleness over being right. Let heaven's wisdom guide your responses.

Reflection Question: Which aspect of heavenly wisdom does your marriage need most?

DAY 314

"He that hath knowledge spareth his words: and a man of understanding is of an excellent spirit." – Proverbs 17:27 (KJV)

Knowing when not to speak is marriage genius. That lecture forming in your mind? Spare those words. That "I told you so" dancing on your tongue? Swallow it. Knowledge knows; wisdom withholds.

An excellent spirit doesn't need to prove itself right constantly. It can watch your spouse learn without saying "I knew that would happen." It can spare words because it values peace over points.

Use fewer words today. See if excellence follows.

Reflection Question: What words need sparing for spirit's sake?

DAY 315

"Let nothing be done through strife or vainglory; but in lowliness of mind let each esteem other better than themselves." – Philippians 2:3 (KJV)

Who gets credit in your marriage? Who's the hero of your stories? If it's always you, vainglory might be driving. Lowliness of mind doesn't mean thinking less of yourself—it means thinking of yourself less.

Esteem your spouse better in practical ways. Give them the credit. Let them tell the story. Celebrate their victory without mentioning your contribution. It's not about being a doormat but about being a spotlight that illuminates them.

Make them the star today.

Reflection Question: How can you esteem your spouse above yourself practically?

DAY 316

"The aged women likewise... may teach the young women to be sober, to love their husbands, to love their children." – Titus 2:3-4 (KJV)

Love is learned behavior. You didn't automatically know how to love your specific spouse with their specific needs. Someone taught you—through example, advice, or counterexample of what not to do.

Find mentors who've loved well for decades. Learn from their victories and mistakes. But also recognize you're teaching others by your example. Some couple is watching you for hope or warning. Make sure they're learning love, not dysfunction.

Keep learning, start teaching.

Reflection Question: Who's teaching you to love better, and who's learning from you?

DAY 317

"And let us consider one another to provoke unto love and to good works." – Hebrews 10:24 (KJV)

Provoking usually sounds negative, but here it's beautiful—intentionally stirring up love and good works in your spouse. You know their buttons; push the right ones.

What provokes your spouse to love? Maybe it's when you appreciate their efforts. What stirs them to good works? Perhaps it's when you believe in their dreams. Be intentional about provoking their best, not their worst.

You have incredible influence—use it for good.

Reflection Question: How can you provoke love in your spouse today?

DAY 318

"A prudent wife is from the LORD." – Proverbs 19:14 (KJV)

Prudence—wisdom in action—is God's gift to marriage. When your spouse shows prudence (and they do, even if you don't always see it), that's divine provision. God is protecting you through their wisdom.

Maybe they're prudent with money while you're spontaneous. Perhaps they're cautious where you're risky. That prudence that sometimes frustrates you? It's from the LORD, designed to balance and bless. Both spouses bring different prudence to marriage.

Thank God for your spouse's prudence.

Reflection Question: What prudence does your spouse bring that you've been resisting?

DAY 319

"Wherefore comfort yourselves together, and edify one another, even as also ye do." – 1 Thessalonians 5:11 (KJV)

Your spouse faces battles you don't see—internal struggles, workplace pressures, family dynamics. They need your comfort more than your criticism, your edification more than your evaluation.

Comfort says, "That sounds really hard." Edification says, "I see how well you handled that." Together, they create an atmosphere where your spouse can be vulnerable about struggles and celebrated for victories. Be their safe place to fall and their launching pad to rise.

Comfort and edify intentionally today.

Reflection Question: Does your spouse need more comfort or edification right now?

DAY 320

"Be not overcome of evil, but overcome evil with good." – Romans 12:21 (KJV)

When your spouse is being difficult (evil is strong, but you get the point), you have two choices: be overcome or overcome. Match their negativity and both sink, or respond with good and both rise.

It's like martial arts—using their negative energy against itself. They're grumpy? Respond with unusual kindness. They're critical? Counter with compliments. They're distant? Move closer. Good overcomes evil every time, but you have to deploy it.

Overcome today's evil with unexpected good.

Reflection Question: What evil in your marriage needs good to overcome it?

DAY 321

"For ye have need of patience, that, after ye have done the will of God, ye might receive the promise." – Hebrews 10:36 (KJV)

You've been working on your marriage—praying, serving, forgiving, trying. Where's the breakthrough? Why isn't change happening faster? Welcome to the waiting room between obedience and promise.

Patience isn't passive—it's actively trusting while waiting. Like a farmer who plants, waters, then waits. The harvest is coming, but not on your timeline. Keep doing God's will in your marriage. The promise is as certain as His word.

Don't give up five minutes before the miracle.

Reflection Question: What promise are you patiently waiting to see fulfilled?

DAY 322

"How much better is it to get wisdom than gold!" – Proverbs 16:16 (KJV)

You could win the lottery tomorrow, but without wisdom, your marriage would still struggle. Wisdom knows how to navigate conflict, build intimacy, and create lasting love. Gold just pays bills.

Invest in wisdom for your marriage. Read books together. Seek counseling. Learn from others. Watch couples who've succeeded. Wisdom compounds interest better than any investment. It pays dividends in peace, joy, and connection.

Choose wisdom over wealth.

Reflection Question: What wisdom investment could strengthen your marriage?

DAY 323

"Put on therefore, as the elect of God, holy and beloved, bowels of mercies, kindness, humbleness of mind, meekness, longsuffering." – Colossians 3:12 (KJV)

Getting dressed for marriage means putting on the right attributes. Not clothes but character. Every morning, dress your heart in mercy, kindness, humility, meekness, and patience.

Imagine if you approached your spouse wearing kindness like cologne, mercy like jewelry, humility like your favorite outfit. These aren't natural clothing—you have to purposely put them on. They don't just happen; you choose them.

Dress for marriage success.

Reflection Question: Which attribute do you most often forget to put on?

DAY 324

"Even so must their wives be grave, not slanderers, sober, faithful in all things." – 1 Timothy 3:11 (KJV)

Faithfulness in all things—not just the big things but the boring things. Faithful in daily kindness. Faithful in keeping confidences. Faithful in small promises. Both spouses need this comprehensive faithfulness.

Slander destroys marriages—not just lies but truth shared wrongly. That venting to friends about your spouse? That's slander. That complaint disguised as prayer request? Slander. Be grave (serious) about protecting your spouse's reputation.

Be faithful in everything, especially the small things.

Reflection Question: Where does your faithfulness need to expand?

DAY 325

"Giving thanks always for all things unto God." – Ephesians 5:20 (KJV)

"All things" includes your spouse's weakness that makes you stronger. Their different perspective that broadens yours. Even their struggles that teach you patience. Gratitude finds gold in everything.

Start a thanksgiving list about your spouse—not just obvious blessings but hidden ones. Thank God for what irritates you (it's growing you). Thank Him for what challenges you (it's changing you). Always, all things—that's comprehensive gratitude.

Thank God especially for the hard things.

Reflection Question: What difficult aspect of marriage deserves thanksgiving?

DAY 326

"Be perfect, be of good comfort, be of one mind, live in peace." – 2 Corinthians 13:11 (KJV)

Perfect here means complete, not flawless. Your marriage is becoming complete—adding comfort where there was conflict, unity where there was division, peace where there was problems.

Being of one mind doesn't mean identical thoughts but unified purpose. Good comfort means encouraging each other toward growth. Living in peace means choosing harmony over having your way. These aren't destinations but daily decisions.

Choose completeness over perfection.

Reflection Question: Which of these four needs most attention in your marriage?

DAY 327

"She stretcheth out her hand to the poor; yea, she reacheth forth her hands to the needy." – Proverbs 31:20 (KJV)

When your spouse is poor—in energy, patience, or hope—do you stretch out your hand or withdraw? Both spouses can be rich or poor depending on the day. Today you have surplus; tomorrow you might have shortage.

Reaching forth requires effort, initiative, and awareness. See where your spouse is needy—maybe for appreciation, affection, or assistance. Don't wait for them to beg. Stretch out your hand while you have something to give.

Be generous when they're needy.

Reflection Question: Where is your spouse poor and needing your generosity?

DAY 328

"Lie not one to another, seeing that ye have put off the old man with his deeds." – Colossians 3:9 (KJV)

Little lies erode big trust. "I'll be home in five minutes" (when you haven't left). "I forgot" (when you didn't try to remember). "Everything's fine" (when it's falling apart). These seem harmless but they're harmful.

You've put off the old man—the one who needed to lie for protection or manipulation. The new you can tell truth because you're secure in Christ and your covenant. Truth might be uncomfortable, but it's less damaging than discovered deception.

Tell truth even when it's hard.

Reflection Question: What little lie needs to become truth?

DAY 329

"Let us therefore follow after the things which make for peace, and things wherewith one may edify another." – Romans 14:19 (KJV)

Every choice either builds peace or breaks it. That tone you're about to use—does it make for peace? That topic you're raising—will it edify? Peace and edification should be your marriage's GPS setting.

Following after means actively pursuing, not accidentally arriving. It's choosing the peaceful approach over the proven point. It's selecting edifying words over devastating ones. Every interaction is a choice toward peace or problems.

Follow peace like it's your job.

Reflection Question: What choice today would make for more peace?

DAY 330

"Now the God of patience and consolation grant you to be likeminded one toward another." – Romans 15:5 (KJV)

Likeminded doesn't mean identical—it means harmonized. Like two instruments playing different notes but the same song. God grants this unity through patience (waiting for each other) and consolation (comforting through difficulties).

You're becoming likeminded every time you choose understanding over argument. Every time you comfort instead of criticize. Every time you wait instead of rush. God is granting what you're receiving.

Receive the gift of becoming likeminded.

Reflection Question: Where is God creating likemindedness in your differences?

DAY 331

"Looking diligently lest any man fail of the grace of God; lest any root of bitterness springing up trouble you." – Hebrews 12:15 (KJV)

Bitterness starts underground—invisible roots spreading before visible fruit appears. That resentment you're nurturing? It's growing deeper while you sleep. By the time bitterness springs up, it's almost too late.

Look diligently for roots. That comment that stung? Deal with it before it roots. That disappointment? Address it before it spreads. Bitterness is easier to prevent than remove. Your marriage can't afford what bitterness costs.

Do some root inspection today.

Reflection Question: What root of bitterness needs immediate attention?

DAY 332

"Rejoice with them that do rejoice, and weep with them that weep." –
Romans 12:15 (KJV)

Your spouse needs you to match their emotional weather. When they're celebrating, don't rain on their parade. When they're grieving, don't force sunshine. Just be with them where they are.

This requires emotional flexibility—setting aside your mood to enter theirs. They got promoted while you got passed over? Rejoice anyway. They're grieving a loss you don't understand? Weep anyway. Your presence in their emotion matters more than your advice about it.

Match their emotional frequency today.

Reflection Question: Does your spouse need you to rejoice or weep with them?

DAY 333

"Bear ye one another's burdens, and so fulfil the law of Christ." – Galatians
6:2 (KJV)

Your spouse's burden isn't just their problem—it's your ministry opportunity. That work stress, family drama, health concern—you can't fix it, but you can share the weight.

Bearing burdens looks different for each situation. Sometimes it's listening without solving. Sometimes it's taking on extra chores. Sometimes it's just being present. Christ bore our ultimate burden; you can bear your spouse's daily ones.

Pick up some of their weight today.

Reflection Question: What burden can you help carry?

DAY 334

"Let all your things be done with charity." – 1 Corinthians 16:14 (KJV)

Everything—from major decisions to mundane tasks—filtered through love. Making dinner? Add love. Discussing finances? Include love. Disciplining children? Mix in love. Love changes everything it touches.

Charity isn't just feeling but action soaked in affection. It's the difference between grudging duty and grateful service. Your spouse can feel whether love motivates your actions or obligation drives them.

As November ends, let love flavor everything like Thanksgiving seasoning.

Reflection Question: What routine task needs love's transformation?

December: The Gift of Presence

Day 335

"Every good gift and every perfect gift is from above, and cometh down from the Father of lights." – James 1:17 (KJV)

December illuminates everything with lights, but the best gift isn't under your tree—it's beside you on the couch. Your spouse is God's good and perfect gift, even when they feel more like a gag gift some days.

Think about it: out of billions of people, God orchestrated circumstances for you two to meet, connect, and commit. That's not accident; that's gift. They're not perfect, but they're perfect for you—custom selected by the Father of lights.

This Christmas season, recognize the gift you already unwrapped at your wedding.

Reflection Question: How is your spouse God's perfect gift for your specific life?

DAY 336

"For unto us a child is born, unto us a son is given." – Isaiah 9:6 (KJV)

God's ultimate gift wasn't wrapped in paper but in humanity. Jesus shows that the best gifts come in unexpected packages. Your spouse might not be the package you ordered, but they're the gift you needed. Maybe you wanted someone more romantic; God gave you someone stable. You wanted adventurous; He gave you safe. Like hoping for a toy and getting socks—boring at first, but essential for the journey. Look past the wrapping to the gift within.

Reflection Question: What unexpected gift did God give you in your spouse?

DAY 337

"Thanks be unto God for his unspeakable gift." – 2 Corinthians 9:15 (KJV)

Some gifts defy description. How do you explain the comfort of your spouse's presence during crisis? The joy of inside jokes? The security of being fully known and still loved? These are unspeakable gifts. Your marriage contains treasures you can't articulate—the way they know your coffee order, sense your moods, finish your sentences. These seem small but they're unspeakably precious. They're evidence of deep knowing, careful attention, and persistent love. Thank God for the unspeakable gifts in your marriage.

Reflection Question: What unspeakable gift does your marriage contain?

DAY 338

"It is more blessed to give than to receive." – Acts 20:35 (KJV)

Christmas can become a scorecard—who spent more, who gave better gifts. But the real blessing comes from giving without counting. Your spouse needs gifts that can't be wrapped—patience, presence, and purpose.

Give what they really want: your undivided attention during their story, your enthusiasm for their interests, your support for their dreams. These gifts cost more than money (they cost self), but they bless more than anything from a store.

Give yourself—it's what they really want.

Reflection Question: What non-material gift does your spouse most need?

DAY 339

"And she shall bring forth a son, and thou shalt call his name JESUS: for he shall save his people from their sins." – Matthew 1:21 (KJV)

Jesus came to save from sin, including the sins that threaten marriages—selfishness, unforgiveness, pride. His birth brings hope for your relationship's rebirth. What seems dead can resurrect.

Your marriage sins—the harsh words, cold shoulders, broken promises—don't have to define your future. Jesus saves from sin's penalty and power. That pattern you can't break? He can. That hurt you can't heal? He will.

Let Christmas remind you: salvation is available.

Reflection Question: What marriage sin needs Jesus' saving power?

DAY 340

"And the Word was made flesh, and dwelt among us." – John 1:14 (KJV)

God didn't send a memo; He sent Himself. He dwelt among us—close, touchable, present. Your marriage needs that same incarnational love—not distant good wishes but present participation.

Dwell with your spouse, not just in the same house but in the same emotional space. Enter their world. Learn their language. Become flesh—real, vulnerable, and available. Don't just tell them you love them; show up in their reality.

Make your love incarnate—word made flesh.

Reflection Question: How can you better dwell in your spouse's world?

DAY 341

"For mine eyes have seen thy salvation." – Luke 2:30 (KJV)

Simeon waited years to see salvation. You might be waiting to see salvation in your marriage—that breakthrough, that healing, that change. Keep your eyes open; salvation often comes in unexpected ways.

Maybe salvation looks like your spouse finally opening up. Perhaps it's you finally letting go. Salvation might not look like you imagined—it rarely does. But when you see it, you'll know it.

Keep watching. Your eyes will see salvation.

Reflection Question: What salvation are you waiting to see in your marriage?

DAY 342

"Glory to God in the highest, and on earth peace, good will toward men." – Luke 2:14 (KJV)

The angels announced peace on earth, starting with your address. Your marriage can be ground zero for God's peace project. But peace requires good will—choosing to think the best, assume positive intent, and extend grace.

Good will toward your spouse means interpreting their actions generously. They forgot milk? Maybe they're overwhelmed, not thoughtless. They're quiet? Perhaps processing, not punishing. Good will changes everything.

Let peace begin in your home.

Reflection Question: Where does your marriage need more good will?

DAY 343

"And they came with haste, and found Mary, and Joseph, and the babe lying in a manger." – Luke 2:16 (KJV)

The shepherds came with haste—urgently, immediately, dropping everything. When did you last approach your spouse with that kind of urgency? Not panic but priority. Not crisis but intention.

Come to your marriage with haste today. Don't delay that apology. Don't postpone that affection. Don't defer that difficult conversation. Some things shouldn't wait for convenient timing. Approach your spouse like the shepherds approached Jesus—eagerly.

Reflection Question: What needs your urgent attention in your marriage?

DAY 344

"When they saw the star, they rejoiced with exceeding great joy." – *Matthew 2:10 (KJV)*

The wise men's journey was long, difficult, and uncertain. Then they saw the star—confirmation they were heading right. Your marriage journey has those moments too—confirmations that you chose right.

Maybe it's how they held you during grief. How they celebrated your success. How they stayed when leaving would've been easier. These are stars—bright moments confirming you're on the right path together.

Rejoice in your confirmation moments.

Reflection Question: What recent "star" confirmed you're on the right path?

DAY 345

"And when they were come into the house, they saw the young child with Mary his mother, and fell down, and worshipped him." – *Matthew 2:11 (KJV)*

The wise men's gifts were secondary to their worship. Your spouse needs your worship of God more than your presents. A spouse who truly worships God becomes a better partner—more humble, gracious, and loving.

When you both fall down before God, you rise up better for each other. Worship changes worshippers. Let your spouse see you worship—not performing but genuinely surrendering to God. Worship together. It's the best gift you can give.

Reflection Question: How could worshipping together strengthen your marriage?

DAY 346

"For unto you is born this day in the city of David a Saviour, which is Christ the Lord." – Luke 2:11 (KJV)

"Unto you"—personal, specific, and direct. Christ wasn't born for humanity in general but for you specifically. For your marriage particularly. For your struggles personally.

This day—every day—Christ is available as Saviour for your marriage. Saving it from selfishness, bitterness, and brokenness. He's not distant deity but present help. Your marriage has a Saviour; use Him.

Make it personal: Christ came for your marriage.

Reflection Question: How does your marriage need Christ as Saviour today?

DAY 347

"And she brought forth her firstborn son, and wrapped him in swaddling clothes, and laid him in a manger; because there was no room for them in the inn." – Luke 2:7 (KJV)

No room in the inn, but God still worked His plan. Your marriage might feel like a stable sometimes—not ideal, slightly messy, definitely not Instagram-worthy. But God births beautiful things in imperfect places.

Stop waiting for perfect conditions to let God work. He specializes in stables. Your less-than-ideal marriage is exactly where miracles can happen. Make room for Him even when circumstances are cramped.

God works in marriages that feel like stables.

Reflection Question: What miracle can God birth in your imperfect situation?

DAY 348

"Now when Jesus was born in Bethlehem of Judaea in the days of Herod the king, behold, there came wise men from the east." – Matthew 2:1 (KJV)

The wise men traveled far to find Jesus. How far would you travel for your marriage? Not physically but emotionally—leaving comfort zones, crossing into vulnerability, journeying through difficult conversations.

Wise people go the distance for what matters. They don't let distance, difficulty, or duration stop them. Your marriage is worth the journey, even when the star seems distant.

Be wise. Make the journey.

Reflection Question: What distance do you need to travel for your marriage?

DAY 349

"And the angel said unto them, Fear not: for, behold, I bring you good tidings of great joy." – Luke 2:10 (KJV)

Fear not—easier said than done in marriage. Fear of failure, repetition of past patterns, or future uncertainties. But good tidings are coming. Great joy is available. The angel's message is for your marriage too.

What are you fearing that's stealing your joy? That financial pressure? Fear not. That parenting challenge? Fear not. That health concern? Fear not. Good tidings often come disguised as difficulties.

Exchange fear for joy.

Reflection Question: What fear needs replacing with joy?

DAY 350

"And Joseph also went up from Galilee... To be taxed with Mary his espoused wife, being great with child." – Luke 2:4-5 (KJV)

Joseph had every reason to complain—taxes, travel, pregnant wife, no reservations. But he went anyway, stayed anyway, loved anyway. Sometimes marriage requires doing hard things without complaint.

Your spouse needs a Joseph—someone who shows up even when circumstances are difficult. Who travels hard roads together. Who doesn't abandon ship when storms hit. Be that steady presence.

Show up like Joseph—faithful despite difficulty.

Reflection Question: Where does your spouse need your Joseph-like faithfulness?

DAY 351

"And suddenly there was with the angel a multitude of the heavenly host praising God." – Luke 2:13 (KJV)

Heaven couldn't contain its praise at Christ's birth. When did your marriage last inspire praise? Not perfection but praise for progress, for perseverance, for presence.

Create praise moments in your marriage. Celebrate small victories like heaven celebrates. Make your home a place where praise suddenly breaks out—for God's goodness, for each other's growth, for grace that covers.

Let praise interrupt your routine.

Reflection Question: What deserves sudden praise in your marriage?

DAY 352

"And all they that heard it wondered at those things which were told them by the shepherds." – Luke 2:18 (KJV)

The shepherds told everyone about their encounter. What story is your marriage telling? Are people wondering at God's work in your relationship or wondering why you stay together?

Your marriage is a testimony others are reading. Make it wonderful—not perfect but full of wonder at God's grace. Let others see how God transforms ordinary people into extraordinary partners.

Tell a story worth wondering at.

Reflection Question: What wonderful story is your marriage telling?

DAY 353

"But Mary kept all these things, and pondered them in her heart." – Luke 2:19 (KJV)

Some marriage moments need pondering, not posting. Those sacred exchanges, private victories, and intimate revelations—keep them, treasure them, ponder them. Not everything needs an audience.

Your spouse needs to know some things are just between you two (and God). That their vulnerability is safe. That sacred moments stay sacred. Be like Mary—a keeper and ponderer of precious things.

Keep some things just for your heart.

Reflection Question: What precious moment needs pondering, not publicizing?

DAY 354

"Where is he that is born King of the Jews? for we have seen his star in the east, and are come to worship him." – Matthew 2:2 (KJV)

The wise men asked questions and followed stars. Your marriage needs both—honest questions about where you're going and willingness to follow divine guidance to get there.

"Where is our marriage heading?" "What star are we following?" Don't be afraid of questions; they lead to discoveries. Follow the star of God's purpose for your relationship, even when the journey seems long.

Keep asking, keep following.

Reflection Question: What question about your marriage needs asking?

DAY 355

"And when they had opened their treasures, they presented unto him gifts; gold, and frankincense, and myrrh." – Matthew 2:11 (KJV)

The wise men brought their treasures—valuable, thoughtful, and significant. What treasures are you bringing to your marriage? Not just material gifts but treasures of time, attention, and affection.

Gold represents value—show your spouse they're valuable. Frankincense represents worship—include God in your marriage. Myrrh represents sacrifice—give what costs you something. Open your treasures generously.

Present your best gifts to your marriage.

Reflection Question: What treasure does your marriage need you to open?

DAY 356

"Being warned of God in a dream that they should not return to Herod, they departed into their own country another way." – Matthew 2:12 (KJV)

Sometimes God redirects your marriage path. That plan you had? He might warning you to go another way. Not backward but different. The wise men's obedience to divine redirection saved lives.

Don't be so committed to your route that you miss God's redirection. Maybe He's warning you away from certain patterns, people, or plans. Going another way isn't failure; it's wisdom.

Be open to divine redirection.

Reflection Question: What might God be redirecting in your marriage?

DAY 357

"And the child grew, and waxed strong in spirit, filled with wisdom: and the grace of God was upon him." – Luke 2:40 (KJV)

Your marriage is still growing, waxing strong, being filled with wisdom. It's not full-grown yet. Give it grace to develop, time to mature, space to strengthen.

Like Jesus grew gradually, your relationship grows daily—sometimes imperceptibly but always purposefully. The grace of God is upon your marriage, enabling growth you can't force.

Celebrate growth, however slow.

Reflection Question: How has your marriage grown stronger this year?

DAY 358

"And when eight days were accomplished for the circumcising of the child, his name was called JESUS." – Luke 2:21 (KJV)

Names matter. What are you calling your marriage? Difficult? Broken? Or blessed? Becoming? Your words name your reality.

God named His Son before birth—purposeful, intentional, and meaningful. Name your marriage what you want it to become, not what it currently appears. Call it blessed, growing, and graced.

Speak life through the names you use.

Reflection Question: What new name does your marriage need?

DAY 359

"And, behold, the star, which they saw in the east, went before them, till it came and stood over where the young child was." – Matthew 2:9 (KJV)

The star kept moving until it reached its destination. Your marriage is still in motion, still being guided, still heading toward God's purpose. You're not there yet, but you're not where you were.

Don't stop following just because the journey's long. The star is still leading. God is still guiding. Your destination—a marriage that glorifies Him—is worth the journey.

Keep following the star.

Reflection Question: How is God still leading your marriage forward?

DAY 360

"And when they were departed, behold, the angel of the Lord appeareth to Joseph in a dream." – Matthew 2:13 (KJV)

God kept speaking to Joseph throughout the journey—warning, directing, and confirming. He's still speaking to your marriage. Through His word, through wisdom, through whispers to your spirit.

Stay listening. Divine communication often comes in quiet moments, unexpected ways, and through your spouse. God hasn't stopped speaking; we've often stopped listening.

Keep your ears open for divine direction.

Reflection Question: What might God be saying to your marriage?

DAY 361

"And he came and dwelt in a city called Nazareth: that it might be fulfilled which was spoken by the prophets." – Matthew 2:23 (KJV)

Even dwelling in Nazareth (the "wrong side of the tracks") was fulfilling prophecy. Your marriage's current location—emotionally, financially, spiritually—might be exactly where God wants you for His purposes.

Stop despising your Nazareth. God uses unlikely places to fulfill His promises. Your humble circumstances, your ordinary life, your imperfect marriage—it's all material for His miracles.

Dwell where God places you.

Reflection Question: How might your current situation be fulfilling God's purpose?

DAY 362

"But when Herod was dead, behold, an angel of the Lord appeareth in a dream to Joseph in Egypt." – Matthew 2:19 (KJV)

Some threats to your marriage will die naturally—that temptation loses power, that conflict resolves, that season ends. Herod couldn't threaten forever. Neither can your marriage's current enemy.

Wait in your Egypt if necessary, but know it's temporary. God will tell you when it's safe to move forward. Some battles you don't have to fight—time and God handle them.

Your Herod won't last forever.

Reflection Question: What threat to your marriage might be naturally dying?

DAY 363

"Then Herod, when he saw that he was mocked of the wise men, was exceeding wroth." – Matthew 2:16 (KJV)

Not everyone will celebrate your marriage's blessings. Some people get "exceeding wroth" when you don't follow their script, when your marriage survives what killed theirs, when you choose each other over their opinions.

Don't let others' wrath determine your direction. The wise men avoided Herod; you can avoid toxic influences. Protect your marriage from those who'd destroy it—even family or friends. Guard your blessing from others' bitterness.

Reflection Question: Whose negative influence needs avoiding?

DAY 364

"In those days came John the Baptist, preaching in the wilderness of Judaea, And saying, Repent ye: for the kingdom of heaven is at hand." – Matthew 3:1-2 (KJV)

As this year ends, repentance prepares for what's coming. Repent of marriage selfishness, negligence, and pride. The kingdom of heaven is at hand—available for your marriage, ready to transform.

Don't carry this year's failures into next year. Repent, receive forgiveness, and restart. Your marriage can be different because the kingdom of heaven is near—closer than you think.

Prepare through repentance for coming blessing.

Reflection Question: What needs repentance before the new year?

DAY 365

"Therefore the Lord himself shall give you a sign; Behold, a virgin shall conceive, and bear a son, and shall call his name Immanuel." – Isaiah 7:14 (KJV)

Immanuel—God with us. That's the promise for your marriage as this year ends and another begins. God WITH you. Not distant, not disinterested, but present in your marriage.

Through every season you've read about this year, through every struggle and celebration, Immanuel has been there. He's still there. He'll be there tomorrow, next year, and every year you have together.

God is with your marriage. That changes everything.

Reflection Question: How has Immanuel been with your marriage this year?

OUR BOOKS

Start each day with purpose, peace, and spiritual renewal.

Whether you're walking solo, side by side with a partner, or seeking strength for the journey ahead—this devotional series meets you right where you are.

Collect the Whole Series

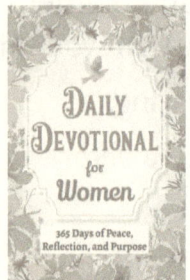 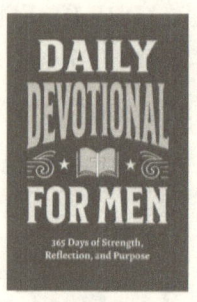 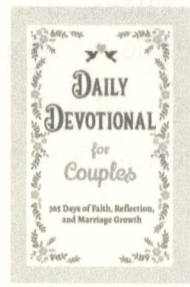

Daily Devotional for Women **Daily Devotional for Men** **Daily Devotional for Couples**

Available at:

- Amazon

- Barnes & Noble

- Major online bookstores

Each book is a spiritual companion. Together, they form a complete journey—personal, relational, and transformative.

Don't wait—bring home the full devotional set and let every day draw you closer to faith, love, and lasting renewal.